Sit a Bit:

Five-Minute Meditations for Greater Health, Harmony, and Happiness

Victor M. Parachin

D1637355

OZARK
MOUNTAIN
PUBLISHING

PO Box 754, Huntsville, AR 72740
479-738-2348; 800-935-0045; fax 479-738-2448
www.ozarkmt.com

For permission, or serialization, condensation, adaptions, or for our catalog of other publications, write to Ozark Mountain Publishing, P.O. Box 332, West Fork, AR 72774 Attn.: Permission Department.

Library of Congress Cataloging-in-Publication Data
Parachin, Victor M. 1946 -
    Sit A Bit – 5 Minute Meditations for Greater Health, Harmony and Happiness by Victor M. Parachin
        Easy meditations for every situation. Answers to many questions about meditation.

1. Meditation   2. Relaxation   3. Centered   4. Health
I. Parachin, Victor M., 1946 -   II. Meditation   III. Title

Library of Congress Catalog Card Number: 2012948712

ISBN: 978-1-886940-34-5
Cover Art and Layout: www.enki3d.com
Book Set in : Times New Roman; Verdana
Book Design: Julia Degan

Published By

P.O. Box 754
Huntsville, AR 72740
WWW.OZARKMT.COM

Printed in the United States of America

Table of Contents

Forward

A meditation teacher was invited to introduce meditation to a group of high school seniors. At the beginning of the class, he asked students to check their resting heart rates by taking their pulse. The instructions were simple:

1. Place two fingers at the base of your thumb on the opposite hand and count the number of pulses you feel in fifteen seconds.
2. Multiply this number by four. This will be your and heart rate in beats per minute.
3. Write down that number.

Next, the students were told they would all meditate for three minutes by following these instructions:

1. Close your eyes and focus on your breathing saying "in" on your inhalation and "out" on your exhalation.
2. Your meditation mantra is just that simple: the repetition of "in" and "out" with each inhale and exhale.

The students stopped after three minutes and again measured their heart rates. Nearly all the students reported a reduced heart rate—anywhere from three to seven beats per minute. That physiological change took place among first time meditators who practiced for a mere three minutes. That's the good news about meditation: you don't have to become a monk on a mountain spending hours in daily meditation in order to gain from it. As the high school students discovered, the benefits of meditation can come after just a few minutes of practice.

In this book you will find 5 minute meditations and methods, which can truly transform your life. You can do these in your own home, at work, even on a train, bus, or subway while on your daily commute. All it takes is 5 minutes—and an open mind. You will lower stress, increase peace, deepen concentration, and live a life of health, harmony, and happiness.

Victor M. Parachin

Introduction

Starting Point: Defining and Demystifying Meditation

There is an abundance of myths and misconceptions about meditation. The most common one is that mediation is complex, esoteric, and time-demanding. The reality is that mediation is easily accessible. Anyone can do it, and it is rewarding to all. Here are some Frequently Asked Questions (FAQs) and answers about meditation that define and demystify this ancient practice.

What is meditation?

Raise this question in a meditation group, and almost every person will answer differently. Some will say that meditation is paying attention, a tool for stress reduction, stilling the mind, a devotional exercise, concentration on spiritual matters, focusing the mind, etc. What this reveals is that meditation can mean different things to different people. No answer is incorrect and no answer is complete. A generic definition which I like is meditation is a process leading to clarity, confidence, serenity, and bliss.

Why do people meditate?

There are as many reasons that people meditate as there are meditators. However, knowing why people meditate can help you reach your goal. There are ten common reasons:

1. *Improved health*—studies show that meditation lowers blood pressure, reduces cholesterol, mitigates migraines, reduces the heart rate, lowers anxiety, and improves energy.
2. *Improved performance*—some athletes meditate and visualize in order to succeed in their sports while other people simply want to be more efficient, get along better with others, work with more focus, and decrease self-criticism.
3. *Deepened creativity*—some people recognize they hold themselves back so they turn to meditation in order to cease censoring themselves in a negative way with thoughts like "I can't do that," "I could never accomplish that," or "I fail at everything I try." Meditation helps these people deepen their creativity by increasing trust in their intuition, improving their confidence, and generating courage to move forward.
4. *Deepened spirituality*—those on a spiritual path turn to meditation in order to directly experience the Divine or the Higher Self; to sense Divine guidance or wisdom; to experience release from past pains, memories, and negative habits; and/or to feel more connected to nature and to others.

5. *Decreased anger*—some people find themselves in circumstances, which make experiencing calm and serenity difficult, if not impossible. Their environment is harsh, upsetting, and anger-inducing.
6. *Curiosity*—this is the individual who has heard about meditation and its benefits and has the courage to try something new.
7. *Managing depression*—many approach meditation to help with depression that may be due to dissatisfaction with life or the result of trauma.
8. *Reduced anxiety and fear*—for some, the unpredictability of life generates anxieties and fears, and meditation is a tool for developing greater emotional balance.
9. *Pain management*—whether it is chronic physical pain or profound psychological scarring, people sometimes turn to mediation for the pain relief it can bring.
10. *Stress reduction*—meditation is not only a proven stress-reliever but can provide insights into ways to change one's circumstances so there is less daily stress.

Can anybody meditate?

Yes. No special skill or equipment is necessary.

What are the benefits?

Thousands of scientific studies have been done, all pointing out that meditation delivers physical, emotional, mental, and spiritual benefits. Briefly, here are some specific benefits:

1. *Psychological benefits:* greater emotional stability; improved mental health; less anxiety, stress, and depression; creative insights; stronger concentration.
2. *Physical benefits:* lower blood pressure; increased energy; speedier recovery from injury and illness; pain relief.
3. *Spiritual benefits:* heightened awareness of something greater than oneself; increased joy, love, compassion, forgiveness; stronger connection to the Divine. Overall, meditation brings peace, wisdom, and joy to daily living.

Why does meditation reduce stress?

We think too much. Thoughts drain energy. When we are awake, usually around sixteen hours per day, our minds are constantly engaged. Even when we sleep, we often dream, so there is no relief from the onslaught of thinking. This in itself is tiring. Then, add this fact: thoughts are seldom neutral. Generally our thoughts attach themselves to emotions, and the most common emotions we experience are fear, anger, anxiety, and desire. Thoughts and emotions are like strips of Velcro, sticking together. It is the thought connected to an emotion which exhausts and stresses us. Meditation is a way of slowing down the thinking process. As we become more skilled in the art of meditation, we can separate the thought from the emotion. Rather than react emotionally to an issue, meditation helps us respond skillfully to life.

Does meditation conflict with my Christian beliefs?

Not at all. Christians find that meditation is an excellent supplement to their other spiritual practices. While Protestant

Christians have lost sight of meditation, many Catholic and Eastern Orthodox Christians have maintained a tradition of meditation. Here are some facts for Christians to consider:

- Christian meditation is rooted in the Bible and is directly mentioned twenty times.
- The Bible recommends meditation. "Be still and know that I am God." Psalm 46:10 (see also Joshua 1:8).
- Moses spent forty days meditating and fasting (Exodus 24:18).
- Jesus went on a private forty-day silent retreat before starting his ministry (Luke 4:2).
- Meditation has been practiced by many prominent Christians who recommended it to others. Arsenius, a desert father (360-440), said, "Be solitary, be silent, and be at peace." Meister Eckhart, mystic (1260-1327), noted that "In silence we can most readily preserve our integrity." Martin Luther told others to "Be silent to God and let Him mold you. Keep still, and He will mold you to the right shape." Mother Teresa remarked that "God is the friend of silence. Trees, flowers, grass grow in silence. See the stars, moon, and sun, how they move in silence."

How is meditation different from relaxation?

While some activities are relaxing, like reading the paper, watching a comedy, taking a hot bath, etc., they do not offer the benefits of meditation. Other activities which masquerade as mediation are daydreaming, thinking, spacing out, prayer, and sleeping. Unlike these types of activities, meditation involves awareness, concentration, and focus. It is an intentional act designed to tame and manage a wild mind.

Do I need a meditation teacher?

You can learn meditation on your own from books and videos. Along with those, a meditation teacher can greatly help you master the basics, refine the process, and eliminate mistakes. A good meditation teacher will also deepen your practice, so it's definitely helpful to find a spiritual mentor. Meditation teachers usually lead groups. Participating in a meditation class will increase your knowledge, motivate you to practice meditation, and bring new friends into your life.

Where can I find a teacher of a meditation group?

The chances are very good that there's a mediation teacher and group in your community. These can be found through yoga studios, temples, churches, health clubs, community centers and Buddhist or Hindu associations.

Do I have to sit on the floor with my legs crossed?

No. The Buddha taught that meditation could be done sitting, standing, walking, and lying down. Many people living in the West are not comfortable in the traditional Eastern meditation position sitting on the floor with legs crossed. There's nothing wrong with meditating while sitting in a chair. Just be certain that your back is erect and straight with your vertebrae stacked like a pile of bricks. Aligning the spine this way is the most comfortable way to meditate.

Should I meditate with my eyes open or closed?

Meditation traditions vary on this question. Some say to keep the eyes closed to block out distractions. Other say to keep the eyes open to prevent drowsiness and sleepiness. Most people who begin meditation find it helpful to gently close the eyes. If you prefer to meditate with eyes open, then follow the Zen practice of sitting and facing a blank wall. This will keep visual distractions from weakening your meditation.

What can I do to keep from falling asleep during meditation?

When you're having trouble remaining awake during a meditation period, there are three things you can do:

1. Open your eyes and focus your sight on some object.
2. Reposition your body and sit more upright.
3. Stand up and meditate.

When is the best time to meditate?

The time to meditate is a matter of preference. Some like to meditate first thing in the morning. Others prefer to do as their last act of the day. Still others find a mid-day practice helpful. Pick a time of day that works for you and then try to reserve that same time for all your meditation periods. That way meditation will become a regular and important habit, like exercising.

What are the different meditation techniques?

The objective in meditation is to quiet or "empty" the mind. However, to "empty" the mind, we must first fill it with something else.

There are four basic ways to meditate:

1. Repeat a mantra, which is simply reciting a word or short phrase repeatedly, such as *Be still.*
2. Be aware of your breath. This involves counting your breath—an inhalation and exhalation counts as one breath.
3. Focus on an object. For example, gaze upon a candle flame, icon, flower, etc.
4. Experience a guided visualization led by a meditation teacher. This enables you to come into a meditative state of relaxation or peacefulness.

Which is right for me?

There is no "right" meditation technique for everybody. Some techniques work better for certain people while other techniques work better for other people. Some techniques work better on one day than another. The important thing is to remain flexible and open to finding just the right one that works for you. In this book, a variety of methods will be presented to give you exposure and experience with different techniques.

Here are some guidelines for using the meditations in this book:

- Find a quiet place where you won't be interrupted.
- Use a stop watch or timer set for five minutes.
- Sit either on a chair or a cushion on the floor.
- Maintain a straight back.
- Gently close your eyes.
- Take a few inhalations/exhalations.
- Begin meditating.
- Stop after five minutes by gently opening your eyes.

MEDITATION MOTIVATOR

Meditation is power. Whatever you do, meditation can help you do it better.

-Stephen Bodian

Part One:

Five-Minute Meditations to Recharge Your Body

Focus: You are not your body!

Meditation is very good for the body. Recent research and scientific study reveals that meditation offers physical benefits. One of the first to research and report on meditation's positive impact upon the body was Herbert Benson, M. D. Associated with Harvard Medical School and its hospitals, Dr. Benson, a cardiologist, conducted extensive experiments with meditators. His work was published in his classic book, *The Relaxation Response*, in which he notes that a wide variety of physical issues "can be significantly improved or even cured when self-care techniques (meditation) are employed." Dr. Benson's list of conditions, which can be "significantly improved or even cured" is impressive and includes the following:

- angina pectoris (chest pain);
- cardiac arrhythmias (irregular heart beat);
- allergic skin reactions;
- anxiety;
- mild and moderate depression;
- bronchial asthma;
- herpes simplex (cold sores);
- cough;
- constipation;
- diabetes mellitus;
- duodenal ulcers;
- dizziness;
- fatigue;
- hypertension;
- infertility;
- insomnia;
- nausea and vomiting during pregnancy;
- nervousness;

3

- all forms of pain—backaches, headaches, abdominal, muscle, joint, post-operative, neck, arm, and leg;
- post-operative swelling;
- premenstrual syndrome;
- rheumatoid arthritis;
- side effects of cancer;
- side effects of AIDS.

In addition, the brain itself is affected by meditation. A group of Tibetan monks were studied by researchers using brain-imaging technology. Pictures were taken of the monks' brains while they were meditating and then compared with pictures taken of their brains before meditating. The images clearly revealed two changes taking place in blood flow to the brain.

1. The front of the brain where concentration takes place was more highly active during meditation. By simply placing their focus on breath, a mantra, a sound, or visual point, blood flooded the frontal lobe.
2. The parietal lobe (the area directly behind the frontal lobe) revealed decreased blood flow and activity. This area gives us a sense of orientation in space and time. Meditators often describe a feeling of being suspended in space and time while meditating, the image a consequence of the decreased blood flow.

As you meditate, do so with the confidence that there is a discernible and beneficial impact upon your brain, one which also leads to improved concentration and focus.

MEDITATION MOTIVATOR

Meditation is a method by which a person concentrates more and more upon less and less.
The aim is to empty the mind while paradoxically remaining alert.
- John H. Clark

Meditations to Release

One of the most influential modern meditation teachers was the Japanese Zen master, Yamada Mumon (1900-1988). He offered this insight into the mind-body connection: "Rather than give the body relief, give relief to the mind. When the mind is at peace, the body is not distressed." These meditations for rejuvenating the body are intended to enhance the power of the mind to positively influence the body.

Meditation for Connecting with Your Body

Just because we occupy our bodies does not mean we are properly connected to them and understand what our bodies need and want. One simple example is that of a long distance jogger who maintains his daily runs even though there is an injury. He is telling his body, "No pain, no gain" when his body is telling him, "I'm hurt and need a few days off." In a case like this, the phrase "You are not your body" is most noticeable.

Use this meditation to connect with your body. It's done by "talking" to the body and asking it these kinds of questions. Pause to "listen" after you ask each question:

- What can I do for you right now?
- What would nourish you right now?
- Is there something I need to do more for you?
- Is there something I need to do less for you?
- What am I keeping you from doing?

MEDITATION MOTIVATOR

Just still the thoughts in your mind.
It is good to this right in the midst of disturbance.
- Yuan Wu

Counting Breath Meditation

One of the most basic meditation styles is simply to focus on your breath. It's something anyone can do at any time and in any place. Here is how it is done:

- Sit comfortably on the floor or chair.
- Breathe evenly and naturally, in and out using this count:
  ○ Breathe in, counting 1, 2.
  ○ Breathe out, counting 3, 4.
  ○ Breathe in, counting 1, 2.
  ○ Breathe out, counting 3, 4.
- Do this for five minutes.

Once you've become accustomed to this counting breath meditation, you can extend the breathing pattern. For example:

- Breathe in, counting 1, 2, 3.
- Breathe out, counting 4, 5, 6.
- Breathe in, counting 1, 2, 3.

- Breathe out, counting 4, 5, 6.
- Do this for five minutes.

Again, as you get used to this pattern, you can continue to count by expanding and deepening your breathing pattern. Another example:

- Breathe in, counting 1, 2, 3, 4, 5.
- Breathe out, counting 6, 7, 8, 9, 10.
- Breathe in, counting 1, 2, 3, 4, 5.
- Breathe out, counting 6, 7, 8, 9, 10.
- Do this for five minutes.

Five Found Releasing Meditation

An ideal time to use this releasing mediation is when you've had a particularly stressful day or experienced a stressful situation. It's designed to specifically release tension and enable a relaxation response. This entire meditation is made up of these five sentences:

Slow . . . down.
Be . . . still.
Letting . . . go.
Feeling . . . calm.
Choosing . . . joy.

However, this meditation builds minute by minute one sentence at a time in this way:

- **Minute 1**: with each inhalation/exhalation, do the following:

- o Repeat "Slow" as you inhale.
- o Repeat "Down" as you exhale.

- **Minute 2**: with each inhalation/exhalation, do the following:

  - o Repeat "Slow" as you inhale.
  - o Repeat "Down" as you exhale.
  - o Repeat "Be" as you inhale.
  - o Repeat "Still" as you exhale.

- **Minute 3**: with each inhalation/exhalation, do the following:

  - o Repeat "Slow" as you inhale.
  - o Repeat "Down" as you exhale.
  - o Repeat "Be" as you inhale.
  - o Repeat "Still" as you exhale.
  - o Repeat "Letting" as you inhale.
  - o Repeat "Go" as you exhale.

- **Minute 4**: with each inhalation/exhalation, do the following:

  - o Repeat "Slow" as you inhale.
  - o Repeat "Down" as you exhale.
  - o Repeat "Be" as you inhale.
  - o Repeat "Still" as you exhale.
  - o Repeat "Letting" as you inhale.
  - o Repeat "Go" as you exhale.
  - o Repeat "Feeling" as you inhale.
  - o Repeat "Calm" as you exhale.

- Minute 5: with each inhalation/exhalation, do the following:

  o Repeat "Slow" as you inhale.
  o Repeat "Down" as you exhale.
  o Repeat "Be" as you inhale.
  o Repeat "Still" as you exhale.
  o Repeat "Letting" as you inhale.
  o Repeat "Go" as you exhale.
  o Repeat "Feeling" as you inhale.
  o Repeat "Calm" as you exhale.
  o Repeat "Choosing" as you inhale.
  o Repeat "Joy" as you exhale.

MEDITATION MOTIVATOR

Meditation makes you self-reliant and helps you attain the inner strength
you need for dealing with all of life's problems.
- Swami Rama

Meditations to Relieve

The Yogi Who Doesn't Feel Pain During Meditation

Researchers in Japan tested a master meditator who said that pain was blocked when he was in meditation. R. Kagiki and colleagues decided to test him by using a laser to create a pain response in his body. They did this before he meditated and then during meditation. Here's what they found when they did brain imaging. During the non-meditation test his brain engaged in normal pain processing; however, during meditation, there was a significant reduction in all the brain areas normally associated with pain activity. Granted, this man

9

was a master meditator, a level many may not reach. Yet he shows clearly the tremendous potential which meditation can bring to anyone seeking to transform and reduce pain. This research is especially important because it demonstrates that meditation not only interrupts a negative state of mind but actually replaces it with a positive state of mind.

Pain Management Meditations

Far too many people live with acute and chronic pain. The traditional way to deal with pain is via prescriptions and/or over-the-counter pain relievers. While these are generally safe, they treat symptoms and not causes. Often it is the brain itself that needs to be "re-wired" to instruct the body that the pain is gone. Here are some visualization meditations that can help reduce and even eliminate physical pain. Be confident in this meditative process of visualization because it does work, causing both brain and body to respond. For example, everyone has watched a movie in which they were moved to tears of sadness or alternately tears of joy. The viewer doesn't personally know the people involved in the movie. It's often a complete work of fiction. Yet brain, body, and emotions are impacted. Visualization meditation works the same way. Using visualization or imagery, you are taking your mind to another place, a place where there is no pain.

Scientific research verifies that meditation can reduce pain. A study published in the *Journal of Neuroscience* demonstrated that a modest amount of meditation done by beginners was effective in reducing pain by as much as 93%.

For the study, fifteen healthy volunteers who had never meditated attended four, 20-minute classes to learn a meditation technique known as "focused attention." Focused attention is a form of mindfulness meditation where people are taught to attend to their breath and let go of distracting thoughts and emotions. Before and after meditation, the volunteers' brain activity was checked via an imaging process similar to an MRI.

During these scans, a pain-inducing heat device was placed on the participants' right legs. This device heated a small area of their skin to 120° Fahrenheit, a temperature that most people find painful over a 5-minute period.

According to Fadel Zeidan, Ph.D., lead author of the study and post-doctoral research fellow at Wake Forest Baptist Medical Center, the scans taken after meditation training showed that every participant's pain ratings were reduced with decreases ranging from 11% to 93%.

Pain Management Mediation #1

Pain medications are best done with different type of breathing pattern than we have previously discussed—namely, by making the exhalations longer than the inhalations. A good way to measure this is by counting as you inhale and exhale.

Here's an example:

- Inhale as you count up to 4;
- Exhale as you count up to 6 or 8.

The reason for this is to be certain of you exhale all the stale air in your lungs. Being especially intentional about exhaling all the stale air hidden in the lungs facilitates the release of pain.

Do a scan of your body focusing on releasing tension you feel in any place. Where something is tight or tense, simply instruct that part of the body to release and relax.

Think of a happy pleasant place/time—a moment in your life when you felt relaxed and at peace. Rather than simply recalling a memory, place yourself back into the setting. Once there, try to see, feel, hear, and sense as deeply as possible everything about that place which brings happiness and lightness of spirit. Remain with the visualization as long as possible. If concentration is broken, simply and gently return to the image trying to remain there a bit longer.

Pain Management Mediation #2:

Get into a comfortable meditation position by either sitting upright in a chair or lying on the floor. If your chronic pain comes from the back, you may find it more comfortable to do this meditation lying on your back on the floor or bed with your knees supported.

- Begin with inhalations and exhalations. Be sure to exhale longer than you inhale. After a few rounds this way, begin normal breathing.
- Bring your awareness to the pain and discomfort you experience. Become a detached observer of your body and watch the pain.
- Give it a shape—perhaps like a thunderbolt striking or a giant wave washing over part of your body.
- Give it a color. Is it "red hot"? Is it yellowish orange like a burning fire?
- Try to remain detached and impersonal as you observe it but continue to watch it closely.

12

- As you observe the pain, see if you can consciously change what you see.
  - Can the shape be changed from a thunderbolt to staccato-type bolt, which breaks up almost as quickly as it forms?
  - Can the giant wave washing over your body be downsized to a smaller one?
  - Move on to the color and see if you can change it from "red hot" to a cooler blue.
  - Or try changing the yellowish orange burning fire by visualizing the controls on a gas stove and begin turning down the flame from high to low.

Do pain management meditation with complete confidence. Recent research demonstrates that you don't have to be Buddhist monk with years of experience to benefit from pain meditation. Even beginners with minimal experience have shown that their meditation reduces their pain. In the study, researchers mildly burned fifteen men and women in a lab on two separate occasions—before and after the volunteers attended four 20-minute meditation training sessions over the course of four days. During the second time, when the participants were instructed to meditate, they rated the exact same pain stimulus—a 120-degree heat on their calves—as being 57% less unpleasant and 40% less intense on average. "That's pretty dramatic," said Fadel Zeidan, Ph.D., the lead author of the study and researcher at the Wake Forest University School of Medicine in Winston-Salem, North Carolina. Dr. Zeidan noted that the reduction in pain ratings was substantially greater than those seen in similar studies involving placebo pills, hypnosis, and even morphine and other painkilling drugs.

MEDITATION MOTIVATOR

We are taught how to move and behave in the outer world,
but we are never taught how to be still
and examine what is within ourselves.

\- Swami Rama

Meditation and the Body

When any part of your body is malfunctioning or experiencing weakness, use meditation to focus your attention on that area of the body. Here's a simple exercise to prepare you not only to do that but to show you how it works.

As you sit in meditation:

- Place your focus either upon your feet or your hands.
- Imagine that they are becoming warmer.
  - ○ Some start by seeing their feet or hands as a gray color gradually warming.
  - ○ As they warm, they change from gray to a lighter color and on to a glowing soft pink.

This simple exercise works for many people. Try it first. Then apply the same technique to the part of your body that is compromised. For example, if you suffer from a headache, do a meditation which focuses on your head:

My head releases the pain.
My head restores itself.
My head is healthy.

Another example could be a meditation that focuses on your back if it aches:

My back releases the pain.
My back restores itself.
My back is healthy.

Meditation for Insomnia or Sleep Disorder

Since this meditation addresses sleep disorder issues, it's best done lying on your back in your bed at bedtime. Rather than just lying there waiting and hoping for sleep to come, use the time for meditation. Many find that they fall asleep while they're doing the meditation, and that's the point of this one— to help you fall asleep. Try doing it this way:

1. Take a few breaths to begin relaxing.
2. Focus on your heart as you breathe in and out three times.
3. Focus on your left shoulder as you breathe in and out three times.
4. Focus on your left thigh as you breathe in and out three times.
5. Focus on your navel as you breathe in and out three times.
6. Focus on your right thigh as you breathe in and out three times.
7. Focus on your right shoulder as you breathe in and out three times.
8. Continue to repeat the cycle for five minutes—or longer if you feel yourself relaxing and becoming sleepy.

Meditations for Dealing with Cancer

According to the US National Cancer Institute's Surveillance Epidemiology and End Results (SEER) database, nearly 12,000,000 people deal with some form of cancer and the radiation and/or chemotherapy treatments—which greatly add to their physical discomfort. Meditation is a powerful ally in dealing with the physical and emotional stress of cancer and its treatments. In a controlled study of ninety cancer patients who did mindfulness meditation for seven weeks, 31% had fewer symptoms of stress and 65% had fewer episodes of mood disturbance than those who did not meditate. Some studies have also suggested that more meditation improves the chance of a positive outcome. Here are three meditations to use when there is a diagnosis of cancer.

Quietly and slowly repeat these words over and over for five minutes while slowly and evenly inhaling and exhaling.

Meditation #1

> Every day in every way
> my body is healing.
> Every day in every way
> I am getting better.
> Every day in every way
> I increase in strength and wholeness.

Meditation #2

> Love of God, fall fresh upon me.
> Love of God, fall fresh upon me.
> Healing power of God, fall fresh upon me.
> Healing power of God, fall fresh upon me.

Meditation #3

I release all fear.
My treatment is effective.
Healthy cells are growing.
I release all fear.

MEDITATION MOTIVATOR

A good meditation,
even when it is interrupted by occasional nodding,
is much more beneficial
than many outward religious exercises.
- Johannes Tauler

Meditations to Relax

You don't have to escape to relax and renew. Everything you need to do is within, not without, and that's where meditation takes you. It's also the lesson in this story about a humble tailor, a story that appears in various forms in various cultures.

One evening the tailor had a vivid dream about finding a great treasure, one that would provide him with everything he needed. In the dream he was repeatedly assured that there was a treasure, and it rightfully belonged to him. For days he pondered the meaning of the dream and then decided to leave his small village and venture into the world to seek his treasure.

With a small backpack the tailor wandered from one large town to another, earning money by mending clothing. All the time he searched for the treasure that he knew belonged to him.

After several years of fruitless effort, the tailor encountered a woman who was a sage well-known for her wisdom.

He sought her wise advice and after explaining his dream and his searching, the sage said, "Yes, there is a vast treasure which belongs to you and you alone."

Hearing this from her, the tailor's eyes widened with excitement as she continued, "I will tell you how to find it." Then she gave him detailed directions that he carefully recorded.

Leaving her, the tailor began to follow her directions. After many months, he discovered he had been led back to his village directly to his humble hut. The tailor was ecstatic and began to dig through the earthen floor in his one-room abode. There, indeed, he found a vast treasure!

This story is told to teach an important spiritual lesson. We may wander the globe in search of inner peace, joy, wisdom, and happiness, but those very qualities are buried within our own hearts. What we seek doesn't exist in some far-off location outside our reach. It is found in the depths of our being. The "key" for opening the "door" to inner peace, joy, wisdom, and happiness is meditation. Here are some meditations to help you find the treasure of relaxation.

Calm, Peaceful, Relaxed (CPR) Meditation

This CPR meditation, an excellent stress-reliever and body-relaxer, is based on the words *calm*, *peaceful*, and *relaxed*. Simply repeat these sentences over and over while deeply and slowly inhaling and exhaling.

I am calm.
I am peaceful.
I am relaxed.

CPR Mindfulness When Driving

Sadly, road rage is on the increase as more and more people commute to work and for pleasure. While no one should meditate and drive at the same time, the above CPR meditation can be used as a mindfulness moment while driving, especially in heavy, stressful traffic. Rather than allowing anger and frustration to rise along with blood pressure, breathe deeply and slowly as you remind yourself:

I am calm.
I am peaceful.
I am relaxed.

Then drive in a calm, peaceful, relaxed way.

CPR Mindfulness When Flying

Another area of high stress involves airports, security, and flight delays. Flight travel is an ideal time to center oneself and ease the stress by practicing the CPR mindfulness meditation. When entering an airport terminal, you could pause briefly and quietly say to yourself: "Entering this airport, I am calm. I am peaceful. I am relaxed." No matter what transpires after that, remain that way: calm, peaceful, relaxed. Greet the next hours with serenity and strength.

MEDITATION MOTIVATOR

Our findings indicated that regular practice of meditation changes the brain in ways that foster a more positive emotional response to things.
- Dr. Richard Davidson, meditation researcher

Meditation on Joy for Yourself and Others

Eleanor Roosevelt once advised, "Since you get more joy out of giving joy to others, you should put a good deal of thought into the happiness that you are able to give." Here is a meditation to heighten the joy in your life.

Look back over the last seven days—one week—meditatively asking:

1) Where did I experience joy? Pause to ponder carefully.
2) Where did I bring joy? Pause to ponder carefully.
3) Where can I deliver joy? This time look into the next seven days—one week—identifying people and places where you can transmit joy.

Meditation to Re-kindle Joy

We don't have to create joy because it is an innate quality within us. Joy can be experienced at any time and even during difficult moments. We simply need to find ways of tapping into it. Here is a meditation to re-kindle joy in your life:

Sit comfortably and take a few deep inhalations/exhalations. Then return to normal breathing.

- Think back to a time when you experienced a great joy.
- Examine the experience closely and carefully in great detail.
- Quietly ask yourself, "How did this joy feel in my body. . . in my mind. . . in my emotions?"
- Allow those feelings to re-register inside of you.

Over the next few days, continue to recall this joy moment. Use this memory to move you into an uplifted spirit whenever you feel discouraged or disheartened.

MEDITATION MOTIVATOR

A mind too active is no mind at all.

- Theodore Roethke

Meditation Affirming Your True Nature

Many times we're too hard on ourselves and view ourselves as weak, ineffective, hesitant, and timid. That becomes so ingrained in our thoughts that we come to believe it's our true nature. However, Buddhist thought teaches just the opposite. Buddhists like to remind us that whenever we look into a mirror, we are seeing a Buddha. Our true nature is Buddhahood and everything that implies.

One way of actualizing our true nature is to meditate upon it. Sit comfortably and take a few deep inhalations/exhalations. Then return to normal breathing. Then repeat these three statements slowly, carefully, over and over during your five-minute meditation.

- Joy is my true nature.
- Love is my true nature.

21

- Peace is my true nature.

You can also get creative and change the descriptions:

- Kindness is my true nature.
- Courage is my true nature.
- Buddhahood is my true nature, etc.

Let Nature Nurture

Nature is a great healer. Researchers are discovering that forests, open air, and other green environments deliver health benefits to participants. One British study worked with people suffering with depression. An amazing 71% of the participants reported decreased levels of depression after something as simple as a "green walk" through a park. Similarly, scientists with the Finnish Forest Research Institute reported that people who spend time in green settings experience lower levels of stress, anger, and aggression while increasing their happiness levels. They say the stress-relieving effects of being in nature are so powerful that they strengthen the body's immune system and increase the number and activity of cells which fight cancer. And, the news gets better as the researchers discovered that those who have stressful life experiences recover better and faster when they allow nature to heal. By spending time outside, they receive faster decreases in blood pressure, heart rate, muscle tension, and stress hormone levels. Here are meditations to be done outside, thereby doubling the health benefits—those from Mother Earth and those from meditation.

MEDITATION MOTIVATOR

We may even derive right instructions from nature, from trees and flowers, from stones and rivers.
- Piyadassi Thera

Nature Meditation with Eyes Open

Always begin meditation in nature by focusing on the sensations of sight, sound, smell, touch, and possibly taste, such as sampling a blackberry growing in the wild. Find a quiet place to sit comfortably. (I like to sit with my back against a tree.)

- Take several deep inhalations and exhalations.
- Begin to breathe normally.
  - Focus on sight. Take in the surrounding—trees, grass, birds, insects, etc.
  - Focus on sounds—birds singing, people talking, walking, jogging, or biking, etc.
  - Focus on smells—flowers, the earth, someone barbecuing, etc.
  - Focus on touch. Place your hands on the earth, feel the tree supporting your back.
- Finish by expressing gratitude to Mother Earth for her beauty.

Nature Meditation with Eyes Closed

Finding a quiet place, sit, and gently close your eyes.

- Take several deep inhalations/exhalations.
- Begin normal breathing.

- With your eyes closed, focus upon a sound—water flowing, a bird singing, a frog croaking, the wind blowing.
- Bring your attention back to a sound if your mind wanders.

Nature Meditation on a Clear Night

Some people enjoy being in nature after dark. On a clear night when you can see the moon and the stars, enjoy this meditation.

- Sit comfortably and take a few deep inhalations and exhalations.
- Begin normal breathing.
- Look at the moon, studying it carefully while noting the light it gives in the darkness.
- Use the moon's light for this personal reflection and ask, "Who are the people who have brought me light in my dark times?"
- Name them one by one and quietly thank them.

A variation of this meditation can be done by focusing on the stars.

- Sit comfortably and take a few deep inhalations/exhalations.
- Begin normal breathing.
- Look at the stars, studying them carefully while noting the light they give in the darkness.

- Use the star light for this personal reflection and ask, "Who are the people who been 'stars' in my life— people who have inspired me to be better and do better?"
- Name them one by one and quietly thank them.

MEDITATION MOTIVATOR

Meditation brings wisdom; lack of meditation brings ignorance.
Know well what leads you forward and what holds you back
and choose the path that leads to wisdom.
- Buddha

Nature Gratitude Meditation

Being outside is an opportunity to witness the abundance of life: birds, trees, insects, animals, leaves, flowers, grasses—all growing and supported by nature. Being in nature is an ideal time to offer this type of gratitude mediation.

- Sit comfortably taking a few inhalations and exhalations.
- Begin normal breath and offer gratitude this way:
  - Inhaling, say: "I am grateful for"
  - Exhaling, say: "the sun which nourishes life."
  - Inhaling, say: "I am grateful for"
  - Exhaling, say: "the rains which nourish life."
  - Inhaling, say: "I am grateful for"
  - Exhaling, say: "the sun and rains which nourish life."
- Repeat these expressions of gratitude over and over, linking the sentences to your inhalations and exhalations.

25

MEDITATION MOTIVATOR

Learning to meditate is the greatest gift you can give yourself in this life.

- Sogyal Rinpoche

Nature Meditation via the Poet Hafiz

Hafiz (1325-1389) was an Islamic Persian poet and mystic who is much loved and admired worldwide. When he was sixty, he began a meditation lasting forty days and nights. He sat in a circle which he drew around himself. It was during that time he had a mystical experience simply described as "cosmic consciousness." This beloved Hafiz poem is well worth meditating upon, especially while in nature.

> Even after all this time,
> The sun never says to the earth,
> 'You owe me.'
>
> Look what happens
> With a love like that.
>
> It Lights the Whole Sky.

Mother Earth Nature Meditation

This one can be done as a walking meditation or, if you prefer, while sitting or lying in nature. Remember to take a few deep inhalations and exhalations. Then return to normal breathing.

Mother Earth, let your peace flow over me.
Mother Earth, let your peace grow in me.
Mother Earth, let your peace glow through me.

An Important Life Lesson from Mother Earth

"In the confrontation between stream and rock, the stream always wins—not through strength but through persistence," noted the Buddha. Whenever you find it hard to keep going because the challenges are discouraging, think about our planet earth. Mother Earth experiences monsoons, tornadoes, hurricanes, wildfires, earthquakes, volcanoes. Each time any of those strikes, earth experiences destruction. And yet, the earth heals herself over time. Grass returns, flowers bloom, young trees grow. Mother Earth knows how to work in harmony with life's circumstances. Persistently and consistently she finds ways to self-heal.

The next time a "disaster" or crisis strikes you:

Be like Mother Earth.
Weather the storms of life.
Take the beating.
Wait patiently for them to pass because they will pass.
Work harmoniously with your circumstances.
Be persevering and persistent.
And then, as soon as possible, begin healing and rebuilding yourself.

Sit a Bit

Part Two:

Five-Minute Meditations to Regenerate Your Mind

Focus: Don't believe everything you think!

Meditation is very good for the mind. Recent research and scientific study reveals that meditation offers these mental benefits:

- Greater creativity;
- Decreased anxiety;
- Less depression;
- Greater self-confidence;
- Improved concentration;
- Increased self-discipline;
- Improved learning ability;
- Stronger memory;
- Increased feelings of vitality;
- More happiness;
- More emotional stability;
- A higher development of intuition;
- Increased productivity.

MEDITATION MOTIVATOR

Consider these words. . . .
meditation,
medicine,
medic,
medication.
They all come from the same Latin prefix "medicus" which
means to care or to cure.
- Victor M. Parachin

Another mental benefit that can be added to this impressive list is this: meditation can shift consciousness. Here's a story which many find hard to believe; yet it's true. A prominent yogi was invited to teach meditation workshops in Texas. Arriving to register on the first day was a tall Texan, complete with a large white cowboy hat, a visibly holstered gun with a pearl handle on his side, and two gorgeous women, one on each arm.

Seeing the yogi, the Texan approached him saying: "I've come here because I'm really interested in meditation, but I want to know if, in doing this, I have to give up guns, women, and liquor. If the answer is 'yes' then I don't want to participate," he said bluntly.

The yogi responded saying that he was there just to teach meditation, adding, "I'm not here to tell you or anyone else how to live or what you have to give up."

The Texan said he was fine with that, registered (with his two girlfriends), and sat through the entire four days of training.

A year later, the yogi was invited back to the same city to offer meditation instruction again. The Texan showed up telling the yogi, "You lied to me last year when you said I wouldn't have to give up my guns, women, and liquor."

Puzzled, the yogi said, "But I never told you to give up anything!"

To which the Texan replied, "Yes, but now that you taught me to meditate, I don't want those things anymore."

After engaging in a regular meditation practice, there was a consciousness shift for the Texan.

Meditation Is a Good Tune-up for Your Brain

Researchers are concluding that regular meditation practice is, in effect, a tune-up for your brain, making it work more efficiently. One study done at the University of Wisconsin noted that people who meditate regularly capture information others miss when presented with a series of visual cues in rapid succession. The difference was even greater with experienced meditators, but even beginners—those who meditated twenty minutes a day—scored better than people who didn't meditate. Just as regular exercise builds strength and stamina, a regular meditation practice improves the brain's efficiency in processing information, as well as enhancing perception and awareness.

Here's something you need to know: your mind is not your friend! Consider this ancient story. Many centuries ago in Japan, a young archer won one contest after another. The young champion experienced a confidence that bordered on arrogance as he boasted incessantly about his skill.

Approaching an elder Zen master, who was well-known for his archery, the young man challenged him to a contest. When they met, the younger man demonstrated his truly remarkable proficiency by hitting the distant bull's eye and then splitting the first arrow with his second shot.

"Old man, see if can match that," he said with both arrogance and disrespect to the elder Zen master.

Undisturbed and without speaking, the master did not draw his bow but motioned for the young man to follow him. Curious, the younger archer followed him to a densely forested mountain area. Finally, the Zen master stopped before a deep, dark, and seemingly bottomless chasm. It was spanned by an old, rotting, and shaky tree, which had fallen across the chasm, forming a flimsy bridge. Calmly stepping out into the middle of the unsteady and potentially perilous bridge, the old master picked a faraway tree as a target. He drew his bow, firing a direct clean hit.

Gracefully stepping off the log he said, "Now it's your turn."

The young archer gingerly stepped out onto the log bridge. Staring in fear at the seemingly bottomless and beckoning abyss, the young man took out an arrow, drew his bow only to completely miss the target.

The Zen master said, "You have much skill with your bow and arrow, but you have little skill with the mind that lets loose the shot."

MEDITATION MOTIVATOR

If I have ever made any valuable discoveries,
it has been due more to patient attention than to any other
talent.

- Isaac Newton

That episode was the Zen master's way of reminding the young archer that the mind can work with us or against us. The mind can be our most powerful ally and or greatest opponent. Meditation is the tool for creating a skillful mind and a brain which works more efficiently. The following mediations will help you train the mind so that it truly becomes your friend.

Meditations to Observe the Mind

Three-Point Mind Observation Meditation

At the end of your day or even at the beginning of a new day, go back and review the previous 24 hours asking yourself:

> What was I thinking? (Then pause to review.)
> Why was I thinking that? (Again, pause to review.)
> What was the result of those thoughts? (Pause again to review.)
> Conclude by reminding yourself, "I am not my thoughts and I have the power to choose and change my thoughts."

NOTE: The problem with our internal dialogue, which is constantly going on, is that it is a mental civil war. Our positive side battles with our negative side. Our intuitive sense is opposed by our rational, logical side, and our generous spirit constantly battles with our self-serving side. It is meditation which halts these constant battles between the lower self and the higher self.

MEDITATION MOTIVATOR

In the confrontation between stream and rock, the stream always wins—
not through strength but through persistence.
- Buddha

Meditations to Challenge the Mind

Meditation Exploring Mind Familiarity

MEDITATION MOTIVATOR

If you place your mind on thoughts that are based upon compassion and wisdom,
that's what the mind will become familiar with.
- Sakyong Mipham Rinpoche

The above quote is provocative because it raises this vital question: "What's my mind 'familiar' with?" If you'd like to begin with our culture, ask the question differently: "What's familiar to the mind of people in our society?"

The answer is as quick as it is obvious: violence, anger, greed, frustration, even rage. These are so "familiar" to the mind that they are easily, quickly, and readily triggered by the smallest of issues. The concepts that are not familiar to the minds of many people in our culture are wisdom, compassion, kindness, civility, etc.

The concept that we become what we think was first taught by the Buddha, who succinctly said, "All that we are is the result of what we have thought. The mind is everything. What we think, we become. "

Building on this ancient Buddhist teaching are the words of the contemporary Buddhist Sakyong Mipham: "If you place your mind on thoughts that are based upon compassion and wisdom, that's what the mind will become familiar with."

This concept of feeding the mind with virtues versus vices also appears in Native American teachings. The story is told of an Elder spending time with his young grandson. The Elder explained to his grandson that all of his life there have been two wolves battling inside of him: "One wolf is prone to anger, hostility, and rage while the other is committed to kindness, compassion, and wisdom."

"Which one will win?" asked the grandson.

"The one which I feed," said the Elder.

Interestingly, this Buddhist concept appears in the Christian Bible as well. The apostle Paul wrote: "You'll do best by filling your minds and meditating on things true, noble, reputable, authentic, compelling, gracious—the best, not the worst; the beautiful, not the ugly; things to praise, not things to curse" (Philippians 4:8-9, *The Message Bible*).

Here is a meditation to explore mind familiarity.

- Sit comfortably and quietly.
- Focus on your breathing for a few moments by saying "In" on the inhalation and "out" on the exhalation.

- Ask yourself, "What is my mind 'familiar' with?"
- Pause to see what comes up: anger or acceptance, greed or generosity, cruelty or kindness.
- Conclude with the resolve to make your mind more "familiar" with virtues association with compassion and wisdom. Do this by repeating affirmations like these:
  o I act compassionately to all.
  o I respond with kindness to all.
  o I see the best in each person.

The 1-21 Meditation for Mind Management

The mind has a mind of its own. Left unchallenged, the mind can lead us astray. Properly tamed, the mind can be our powerful ally. This was something noted by the Buddha, "There is nothing so disobedient as an undisciplined mind, and there is nothing so obedient as a disciplined mind." Thus, an important goal of meditation is to tame and discipline the mind.

One technique for working this way with the mind is the 1-21 mind management meditation. The goal of this meditation is to count up to 21 breaths without any thinking of anything else—without any thoughts entering the mind except for the breath counting.

- Sit quietly and begin to count your breaths with an inhalation/exhalation being one count.
- As soon as a thought enters you mind during the count, it means you have lost the contest with your mind and must, therefore, begin counting over again.
- Do not become discouraged if you only get to the fourth or fifth breath count before your mind wanders

and thoughts enter. This is typical for most people. Be both patient and kind with yourself.

- When you realize you are thinking thoughts, simply acknowledge that this has happened and start the count over beginning at one. With practice you will be able to count more breaths before thoughts emerge.

MEDITATION MOTIVATOR

Within you is the wellspring of Good; and it is always ready to bubble up if you just dig.

\- Marcus Aurelius

Koan Sentence Meditation

A koan is a short statement or story which is much like a riddle. Koans are often used in Zen Buddhism and are designed to force a meditator to "think outside the box." Because a koan statement is odd, unusual, ridiculous, and even bizarre, the meditator must truly focus to come up with an answer. Koans do not have one right answer and can actually have various interpretations. They are excellent ways to challenge the mind. Here some some common Zen koan statements. Pick one and meditate on it for five minutes. Remember to take a few deep inhalations and exhalations first and then return to normal breathing.

What is the sound of one hand clapping?
How do you step from a 100 foot pole?
Can a dog or a cat become enlightened?
How does a goose escape from a long necked bottle?
What is in an empty mind?

Is stillness still?

Is emptiness empty?

What does not exist now?

How can I stop thinking by thinking about stopping thinking?

When you're finished meditating on these koans, write down your answers. Later in the day, tell the koan to a friend or two, asking them for their answers. Then you can compare and see how different personalities can have completely different explanations.

Koan Story Meditation

Meditate on one of these six koan stories. Use them the same way suggested for koan statements.

Koan Story #1

Suiwo, the disciple of Hakuin, was a good teacher. During one summer seclusion period, a pupil came to him from a southern island of Japan. Suiwo gave him the problem "Hear the sound of one hand clapping."

The pupil remained three years but could not pass this test. One night he came in tears to Suiwo. "I must return south in shame and embarrassment," he said, "for I cannot solve my problem."

"Wait one week more and meditate constantly," advised Suiwo.

Still no enlightenment came to the pupil.

"Try for another week," said Suiwo.

The pupil obeyed but in vain.

"Still another week."

Yet this was of no avail. In despair the student begged to be released, but Suiwo requested another meditation of five days, but hey were without result.

Then he said, "Meditate for three days longer. Then if you fail to attain enlightenment, you had better kill yourself."

On the second day the pupil was enlightened.

Koan Story #2

A nun who was searching for enlightenment made a statue of Buddha and covered it with gold leaf. Wherever she went, she carried this golden Buddha with her.

Years passed and, still carrying her Buddha, the nun came to live in a small temple in a country where there were many Buddhas, each one with its own particular shrine.

The nun wished to burn incense before her golden Buddha. Not liking the idea of the perfume straying to the others, she devised a funnel through which the smoke would ascend only to her statue. This blackened the nose of the golden Buddha, making it especially ugly.

Koan Story #3

A Chinese Zen teacher lived alone in a small temple in the country. One day four traveling monks appeared and asked if they might make a fire in his yard to warm themselves.

While they were building the fire, Hogen heard them arguing about subjectivity and objectivity. He joined them and said, "There is a big stone. Do you consider it to be inside or outside your mind?"

One of the monks replied, "From the Buddhist viewpoint, everything is an objectification of mind, so I would say that the stone is inside my mind."

"Your head must feel very heavy," observed Hogen, "if you are carrying around a stone like that in your mind."

Koan Story #4

Hakuin used to tell his pupils about an old woman who had a teashop. He praised her understanding of Zen. The pupils refused to believe what he told them and would go to the teashop to find out for themselves.

Whenever the woman saw them coming, she could tell at once whether they had come for tea or to look into her grasp of Zen. In the former case, she would serve them graciously. In the latter, she would beckon to the pupils to come behind her screen. The instant they obeyed, she would strike them with a fire-poker.

Nine out of ten of them could not escape her beating.

Koan Story #5

Zen students are with their masters at least ten years before they presume to teach others. Nan-in was visited by Tenno, who, having passed his apprenticeship had become a teacher. The day happened to be rainy, so Tenno wore wooden clogs and carried an umbrella.

After greeting Tenno, Nan-in remarked: "I suppose you left your wooden clogs in the vestibule. I want to know if your umbrella is on the right or left side of the clogs."

Confused, Tenno had no instant answer. He realized that he was unable to carry his Zen every minute. He became Nan-in's pupil, and he studied six more years to accomplish his every-minute Zen.

Koan Story #6

The pupils of the Tendai School used to study meditation before Zen entered Japan. Four of them who were intimate friends promised one another to observe seven days of silence.

On the first day all were silent. Their meditation had begun auspiciously, but when night came and the oil lamps were growing dim, one of the pupils could not help exclaiming to a servant, "Fix those lamps."

The second pupil was surprised to hear the first one talk. "We are not supposed to say a word," he remarked.

"You two are stupid. Why did you talk?" asked the third.

"I am the only one who has not talked," concluded the fourth pupil.

MEDITATION MOTIVATOR

True silence is the rest of the mind;
it is to the spirit what sleep is to the body, nourishment and
refreshment.
- William Penn

The 1-5 Exercise

This 1-5 exercise is another Zen breath counting exercise to challenge the mind. It works by counting only five breaths.

- As you inhale, say 1; as you exhale, say 1.
- Next as you inhale, say 2; as you exhale, say 2.
- Continue this process to 5 only,
- Then begin with 1/1, 2/2, 3/3, etc. again.

You'll know you're daydreaming or thinking (not meditating) if you find yourself saying 7/7, 8/8, etc. This is called "automatic counting" and is no longer meditation but daydreaming.

Noise and Sound Meditations

Sometimes during meditation there are sounds and noises: people talking, a TV on, vehicles driving by, construction work taking place, etc. Rather than allow these to become sources of frustration, all noises and sounds can be used for meditation. One example comes from Sen No Riyku (1522-1591) who promoted and perfected the Japanese Tea Ceremony. Evidently during meditation he could hear water dripping into a bowl.

Here is his poem about the drip which reveals how he incorporated the drip, drip, drip into his meditation:

> When you hear the splash
> Of the water drops that fall
> Into the stone bowl,
> You will feel that all the dust
> Of your mind is washed away.

His example is instructive. We can use sounds and noises to deepen our meditation. Some examples:

- If you hear a clock ticking, remind yourself, "Life is precious and short. I will do the best I can with the time I have."
- When you hear people laughing, remind yourself, "It is so good to hear sounds of laughter and joy. I will lighten my life through humor and laughter."
- If you hear the sirens of an ambulance, offer this meditation: "May those who are ill or injured quickly receive medical services. May they recover from their illness or injury."
- When you hear rain coming down, say to yourself, "Just as the rains nourish the planet, my meditation practice nourishes my body, mind, and spirit."

You get the idea. Remember that any sounds or noises you hear can be turned into powerful meditations.

MEDITATION MOTIVATOR

*If you place your mind on thoughts that are based upon
compassion and wisdom,
that's what the mind will become familiar with.*

\- Sakyong Mipham Rinpoche

Meditations to Tame the Mind

One of the earliest pieces of practical advice for mind management was offered by the Chinese Zen Master Pai Chang Huai Hai (720-784 CE). His suggestion is as applicable today as it was then.   Basically, he said to stop trying so hard to control the mind. Rather than do that, be aware of what the mind is trying to do and gently bring it back to meditation. Here's his advice:

> Should your mind wander away, do not follow it, whereupon your wandering mind will stop wandering of its own accord. Should your mind desire to linger somewhere, do not follow it and do not dwell there, whereupon your mind's questing for a dwelling place will cease of its own accord. Thereby, you will come to possess a non-dwelling mind—a mind which remains in the state of non-dwelling. If you are fully aware in yourself of a non-dwelling mind, you will discover that there is just the fact of dwelling with nothing to dwell upon or not to dwell upon. This full awareness in yourself of a mind dwelling upon nothing is known as having a clear perception of your own mind or in other words, as having a clear perception of your own nature.

Huai Hai concludes with one final reminder of what to do when the mind wanders: "When things happen, make no response; keep your minds from dwelling on anything whatsoever. Keep them forever still as the void and utterly pure."

Meditation in a Busy Public Place

A recurring source of our anxiety is self-generated because we have a human tendency to judge our insides by other people's outsides. This takes place almost daily for most of us. For example, we perceive the people around us as calm and happy but experience ourselves as in turmoil and unhappy, or we look at other couples, believing they are happy and content while our own relationship is in need of attention and work. The more we do this, the more we conclude that others "are not like me" or painfully ask, "Why am I so different?"

There is a meditation which can correct this mistaken perception. It is best done in a busy, active place with many people coming and going. A mall is ideal as is a busy airport terminal or even a hospital or doctor's waiting room.

- Enter this public space mindfully.
- Find a place where you can sit and observe (not stare).
- Look around at the people walking by.
- Begin to imagine and understand that many of them feel fearful, anxious, lonely, abandoned.
- Some may even be dealing with serious health issues.
- Build a sense of connection with these strangers by reminding yourself:
  - We are part of a common humanity.

- o We are in this together.
- o We share similar hopes and dreams, fears and anxieties.
- o We are more alike than we are different.
- Conclude by sending this blessing to the strangers walking by you:

> May you be well.
>
> May you be peaceful.
>
> May you feel loved.
>
> May you feel safe and secure.

MEDITATION MOTIVATOR

Like weary waves, thought flows upon thought,
but the still depth beneath is all thine own.
- George MacDonald

A Five-Finger Meditation for Inner Peace, Calmness, & Gratitude

Remember to take a few deep inhalations and exhalations first and then return to normal breathing. Then complete this meditation by using the fingers of one hand.

- Touch thumb to index finger. Recall a pleasant time in your life—a vacation, a romantic dinner, a book which inspired you, a movie which moved you to tears.
- Touch thumb to middle finger. Recall a loving or friendly exchange you had with someone.
- Touch thumb to ring finger. Recall a moment of kindness you have received.

- Touch thumb to pinkie. Recall a time when you felt incredibly joyful and happy.
- Repeat this cycle.

Meditation to Deepen Compassion

To deepen compassion, all that is sometimes necessary is to become aware of the people around you—those whom you encounter regularly but with whom you do not have any special connection or interest. Remember to take a few deep inhalations and exhalations first and then return to normal breathing. Then select one such individual—it could be your coffee barista, a bank teller, grocery store cashier, etc.—and begin to send that person this loving kindness meditation:

> May you be happy.
> May you be fulfilled.
> May you be healthy.
> May you be loved.

Of course, you don't tell the person you are offering this mediation. You just do it and see how quickly you feel a connection to and compassion for people who previously were emotionally invisible to you.

Candle Gazing Gratitude Meditation

Before beginning the meditation, remember to take a few deep inhalations and exhalations and then return to normal breathing.

1. Light a candle . . . gaze at it . . . let the light symbolize those who have been kind/good to you.

49

2. Begin to think of them, one at a time, and the kind ways they treated you—family members, friends, teachers, clergy, strangers . . .
3. As you think of them, quietly use their names, one at a time, saying, "Jim, thank you for being kind to me. Jim, may others be as kind to you . . ."
4. Silently think about someone to whom you can bestow kindness tomorrow or in the next few days.

MEDITATION MOTIVATOR

The moon is one,
but on agitated water it produces many reflections.
Similarly, ultimate reality is one,
yet it appears to be many in a mind agitated by thoughts.
- The Maharamayana

Inner Peace Meditation

Before beginning this meditation to bring greater inner peace and tranquility to your mind, remember to take a few deep inhalations and exhalations and then return to normal breathing. Then slowly repeat these three words:

- Om Shanti: Inhale on "Om" and exhale on "Shanti" (peace).
- Shalom: Inhale on "Sha" and exhale on "lom" (Hebrew for peace).
- Peaceful: Inhale on "Peace" and exhale on "ful."
- Repeat.

Spiritual Non-sectarian Mantra

This simple meditation mantra reminds you that health, happiness, and holiness (or wholeness) are all interlinked. Before beginning this meditation, remember to take a few deep inhalations and exhalations and then return to normal breathing.

Healthy am I.
Happy am I
Holy am I/Whole am I. (This is the recognition of inner-divinity or inner-light or inner-wisdom of one's Higher Self.)

Breath Awareness Meditation

This simple meditation helps us become more aware and focused.

- Sit comfortably—not rigidly—relaxed instead.
- Gently close your eyes.
- Bring attention to your nostrils.
  - o As you inhale, note the subtle flow of cool air entering your nostrils.
  - o As you exhale, note that the air passing out of you is warmer.
  - o Breathe naturally. Don't manipulate the breath in any way. Simple note the cool inhalation and the warmer exhalation.
  - o If your mind begins to drift and thoughts enter, gently acknowledge that you became distracted and bring your attention back to the cool/warm air entering and exiting.

On Eagles' Wings—A Jewish/Christian Meditation

When your mind is filled with anxiety and generating self-doubts about your ability to persevere or overcome a stressful situation, try this mediation based on a text from the Jewish Bible (the Old Testament): "Those who hope in the Lord will renew their strength. They will soar on wings like eagles; they will run and not grow weary; they will walk and not be faint" (Isaiah 40:31, *New International Bible*).

- Begin by reading the verse several times, permitting it to penetrate your mind deeply.
- Pause to take several deep inhalations and exhalations.
- Begin to repeat these four short sentences over and over:

God renews my strength.
I will soar on eagles' wings.
I will run and not grow weary.
I will walk and not be faint.

MEDITATION MOTIVATOR

Give your thoughts a chance to settle down.
Then feel your mind clear like a still forest pool.
- The Buddha

Meditation on the Buddha's Lovingkindness

The Buddha never wrote anything himself, but many wisdom sayings are attributed to him. One of the most popular and one which is studied around the world is his teaching on how to put loving kindness into daily life. Here is one version. For meditation purposes, you can work your way through it by reading a few sentences and then meditating on them.

Loving Kindness (commonly referred to as the Sutra on Lovingkindness)

This is what should be done
By one who is skilled in goodness
And who knows the path of peace:

Let them be able and upright,
Straightforward, and gentle in speech.

Humble and not conceited,
Contented and easily satisfied,
Unburdened with duties and frugal in their ways.
Peaceful and calm, and wise and skillful,
Not proud and demanding in nature.

Let them not do the slightest thing
That the wise would later reprove.
Wishing: In gladness and in safety,
May all beings be at ease.
Whatever living beings there may be;
Whether they are weak or strong, omitting none,
The great or the mighty, medium, short or small,
The seen and the unseen,
Those living near and far away,
Those born and to-be-born,
May all beings be at ease!
Let none deceive another
Or despise any being in any state.

Let none through anger or ill-will
Wish harm upon another.
Even as a mother protects with her life
Her child, her only child,
So with a boundless heart
Should one cherish all living beings:

Radiating kindness over the entire world
Spreading upwards to the skies
And downwards to the depths;
Outwards and unbounded,
Freed from hatred and ill-will.
Whether standing or walking, seated or lying down
Free from drowsiness,
One should sustain this recollection.
This is said to be the sublime abiding.
By not holding to fixed views,
The pure-hearted one, having clarity of vision,
Being freed from all sense desires,
Is not born again into this world.

A Jewish-Christian Meditation on Psalm 23

The 23rd Psalm is possibly the most well-known and beloved text in Jewish and Christian scriptures. It makes an excellent focus for meditation by reading one or two sentences and then meditating upon them:

> The Lord is my shepherd; I lack nothing.
>> He makes me lie down in green pastures.
>> He leads me beside quiet waters;
>> He refreshes my soul.
>> He guides me along the right paths

for his name's sake.
Even though I walk through the darkest valley,
    I will fear no evil
    for you are with me;
    your rod and your staff,
    they comfort me.
You prepare a table before me
    in the presence of my enemies.
You anoint my head with oil;
    my cup overflows.
Surely your goodness and love will follow me
    all the days of my life,
And I will dwell in the house of the Lord
    forever.

MEDITATION MOTIVATOR

Just as a bicycle chain may be too tight,
so may one's carefulness and conscientiousness be so tense
as to hinder the running of one's mind.
-William James

OM Meditation

Chanting OM is an important part of meditation. The ancient yogis became so still and quiet in meditation that they heard a sound at the center of the universe. They identified with that "sound" and began to synchronize themselves with it by humming or chanting OM.

The Greek mathematician, philosopher, and mystic Pythagoras (570-490 BCE) was intrigued by sound and vibration, studying those closely. He believed (what science now confirms) that all forms of matter in the universe emit vibrations. This would be true of the largest, most distant stars to the closest and smallest particles. "All these sounds and vibrations for a universal harmony in which each element, while having its own function and character, contributes to the whole," he wrote.

Physicist Fritjof Capra in *The Tao of Physics* writes, "Rhythmic patterns appear throughout the universe, from the very small to the very large. Atoms are patterns of probability waves, molecules are vibrating structures, and living organisms manifest multiple, interdependent patterns of fluctuations."

Interestingly, today's scientists note that the entire physical universe is made up of energy and vibration. A simple example can be seen via a music store selling instruments. It's been noted that if someone picks up a guitar and plucks the G string, all the other G strings on guitars in the store will begin to vibrate in tune with the first one. Here's another example: if two muscles cells from the heart are extracted, each will initially pulse to its own rhythm; however, if they are placed closely together, they will each beat with the exact same pattern.

So the tradition of simply chanting OM is an important and powerful part of mediation because it's a way of creating vibration and synchronizing with the energy of the universe. Before beginning this OM meditation, remember to take a few deep inhalations and exhalations and then return to normal breathing.

- Note that OM is actually three sounds made up of A-U-M.
- Begin with your mouth open, saying "Ah" then slowly make a smaller circle with your lips to form the "au" sound and conclude by gently bringing the lips lightly together for the "M" sound.
- At that point feel the vibration on your lips, in your nose and nasal passages, your throat, and your chest.
- Chant OM seven times. Then pause and breathe naturally for the same length of time that it took you to chant OM seven times.
- Then return to chanting OM seven more times, followed by the same amount of time for silent meditation.
- Go back and forth this way for five minutes.

MEDITATION MOTIVATOR

Mind is elusive.
You cannot hold it in your hand.
You cannot force it into a test tube.
The only way to know it is to know it from within,
from your witnessing self. . . .
If you want to really understand what the mind is,
then you will have to detach yourself from your mind,
and you will have to learn how to be just a witness.
That's what meditation is all about.
- Osho

Sit a Bit

Part Three:

Five-Minute Meditations to Renew Your Soul

Focus: Harmonize the self with the larger Self!

Meditation is very good for the spirit. Ancient yogis and modern meditators note spiritual/emotional benefits, including:

- emotional, spiritual, and mental detachment;
- peace of mind;
- heightened awareness of the inner self;
- the ability to look beyond the body, mind, and personality;
- living without ego attachment;
- discovery of one's true being;
- attaining self-realization and spiritual awakening;
- maintain a balanced perspective on life.

Before proceeding, it can be helpful to pause and think about the importance of cultivating a broad perspective on your life. Suffering is often deepened because we personalize what has happened. This can leave us feeling victimized by life which, in turn, makes us feel even worse. Maintaining a balanced perspective is what the Buddha helped a woman see in the popular story of Kisa Gotami.

Kisa Gotami approached the Buddha after her daughter died. Shocked, numb, and grieving, she came to the Buddha for help. After listening to her, the Buddha asked if he could think more deeply about how to help her, but in the meanwhile he made this request of her: "Please call in various people and bring me a mustard seed from a home which has never experienced sorrow."

Driven by the hope the Buddha could relieve her sorrow and pain, Kisa began visiting various families asking, "Have you in this household experience sorrow and suffering?" Every home she called on had a sad tale:

> "Yes, my son was forced into military service and never returned."
> "Yes, both my parents were killed when bandits raided our village."
> "Yes, a tree fell on me while farming, and I am paralyzed."
> "Yes, I have been ill for seven years and unable to support myself or my family."

Quickly, Kisa realized that she was not alone in her suffering—that suffering and sorrow can come to all. Kisa returned to the Buddha transformed and became one of his earliest followers.

The question to ponder is this: what happened to Kisa? Obviously, her daughter was still dead, yet Kisa was no longer haunted by that reality. As a result of her search for a mustard seed from a home which had no sorrow, Kisa saw her life in a larger perspective. Her home visits enabled her to understand that life did not single her out for trouble, trauma, and trials. Life happens! Previously she was deepening her suffering by thinking *Why did this happen to me? My child should not have died. Life is so unfair to me,* etc. After the home visits, she was able to accept life the way it was rather than clinging to the way she wanted it to be. Consequently, the pain of grief began to ease and diminish.

As you engage in these meditations to renew your spirit, remember the story of Kisa and the Buddha. Like Kisa, you have a choice in how you will respond to traumas which come your way. Use meditation as a tool for empowering you to respond—not react—to life's difficulties in a rational, healthy, and balanced way.

MEDITATION MOTIVATOR

Through meditation and by giving full attention to one thing at a time,
we can learn to direct attention where we choose.
- Eknath Easwaran

Meditations to Calm

Tibetan Nine Round Breathing Practice

Before beginning this highly effective meditation for calming the mind, remember to take a few deep inhalations and exhalations and then return to normal breathing. Then follow these three steps:

1. For the first three breaths, breathe in through the right nostril and out through the left. Use forefinger to close left nostril when you breathe in and to close the right when you breathe out.
2. For the next three breaths, breathe in through the left nostril and out through the right. Again use forefinger to close left nostril when you breathe in and to close the right when you breathe out.
3. For the last three breaths, breathe in through both nostrils breathing out through both.

63

4. Repeat the pattern for five minutes.

Anger Management Meditation

Anger and impatience often go hand in hand. Here is a meditation to increase patience and decrease anger. It's a simple in/out style of meditation—meaning that you inhale the quality you want more in your life and exhale the one you want less.

- Sit comfortably; gently close your eyes.
- Begin taking several deep inhalations/exhalations.
- Once you've relaxed and entered into the quietness of a meditative spirit, begin reciting these sentences:
  o Relaxation in. Tension out.
  o Patience in. Impatience out.
  o Compassion in. Anger out.
- Continue this process for five minutes.

MEDITATION MOTIVATOR

The affairs of the world will go on forever. Do not delay the practice of meditation.
- Milarepa

Alternate Nose Breathing Meditation/Exercise
(Nadi Shodhana in Sanskrit or literally "channel cleansing")

Ancient tradition holds that nadi shodhana or alternate nostril breathing achieves the following:

1. balances the energy channels on the left and right sides of the spine right and left sides of the brain to allow optimal brain function; and
2. calms the mind and nervous system.

In one recent study, alternate nostril breathing reduced blood pressure in participants. Research published in the "Nepal Medical College Journal" found that a yogic breathing exercise, called pranayama, or alternate nose breathing (ANB), helped to lower diastolic blood pressure, pulse rate, and respiratory rate for thirty-six volunteers who followed a four-week program doing alternate nose breathing daily.

Before beginning this nose breathing meditation, remember to take a few deep inhalations and exhalations and then return to normal breathing.

Directions:

1. Bend the middle and pointer finger down toward the palm using only the thumb and ring finger to alternately close off inhalation/exhalation on either side.
2. Close the right nostril with your right thumb. Let the other fingers point toward the sky.
3. Inhale through the left nostril while mentally counting to five.
4. Close the left nostril with the right pinky and exhale through the right side.
5. Inhale through the right nostril—always inhale through the nostril that you have just exhaled with.
6. Do the alternate nostril breathing for a minimum of five minutes.

An Advantage of Left Nostril Breathing

Before beginning this left nostril breathing meditation, remember to take a few deep inhalations and exhalations and then return to normal breathing. Left nostril breathing can help relieve stress, agitation, feelings of being disturbed, or simply feeling like there's too much pressure in your life.

Directions:

1. Find a quiet, private place where you won't be disturbed.
2. Sit with your spine straight.
3. Use the thumb of your right hand, keeping the other fingers together and pointing straight upward like antennae, and close your right nostril. Begin long in-and-out breathing through the left nostril only.
4. Take a minimum of 26 long breaths—about 2 minutes, working your way up to five minutes.

Sat Nam Meditation to Build Confidence

This meditation comes from the Kundalini Yoga tradition. When done for five minutes or more, it can strengthen confidence while easing anxiety and stress. Sat Nam, which means "to honor truth," is done using the fingers of both hands. Before beginning this meditation, remember to take a few deep inhalations and exhalations and then return to normal breathing.

Directions:

- Sit comfortably.
- Place your hands, palm side up, on your knees.

66

- Make an "O" with your thumb and forefinger on both hands.
- Close your eyes, placing the focus on the "third eye" between and slightly above the eyebrows.
- Begin to chant or say "sa-ta-na-ma" while touching your thumbs to your finger tips like this:
    o "Sa"–touch tips of the thumbs to the forefingers;
    o "Ta"—touch tips of the thumbs to the index fingers;
    o "Na"—touch tips of the thumbs to the ring fingers;
    o "Ma"—touch tips of the thumbs to the pinkie fingers.
- Repeat for the duration of your meditation time.

Kundalini Nose-Mouth Breath Meditation

Yogi Bhajan, who established Kundalini Yoga in the West, taught this meditation, which brings wisdom and clarity. Called *gyan mudra kriya*, it is a simple nose-mouth breath meditation combined with a heart type mudra. Before beginning this meditation, remember to take a few deep inhalations and exhalations and then return to normal breathing.

Directions:

- Sit comfortably.
- Bring hands to chest, resting one palm on the other and with both palms facing the chest.
- Cross the thumbs or have them touch.
- Bring attention to the third eye which is located between the eyebrows and slightly higher.
- Follow this breathing pattern:
    o Inhale through the nose. Then exhale through the nose.

- o Inhale through the mouth as your purse your lips to form an "O" shape like you do when whistling. Then exhale through the mouth.
  - o Inhale through the nose. Then exhale through the mouth.
  - o Inhale through the mouth while remembering to purse your lips. Then exhale through the nose.
- Repeat this pattern for five minutes. (NOTE: Yogi Bhajan recommended repeating this for 11 minutes and then working up to ½ hour.)

MEDITATION MOTIVATOR

Doing nothing is better than being busy doing nothing.
- Lao Tzu

A Jewish Christian Meditation Based on Psalm 46:10

This is considered a Jewish and Christian meditation because it is based on a text from the Jewish Bible (Psalm 46:10 in the Old Testament to Christians); it is popular also among Buddhist meditators. The text is one of the clearest directives to meditate found in the Old Testament, simply instructing: "Be still and know that I am God." This verse has eight words in it. Before beginning this meditation, remember to take a few deep inhalations and exhalations and then return to normal breathing.

- Begin meditating by reciting all eight words as a mantra.

- Then continue and drop the last word in the text with each inhalation/exhalation.
- Pause and take an additional breath after reciting each part.
- Here's how it will "look" mentally as you use it for a 5 minute meditation:

Be still and know that I am God.
Be still and know that I am.
Be still and know that I. . .
Be still and know that. . .
Be still and know.
Be still and. . .
Be still.
Be!

Family Meditation

If you're married and have children, you have your own built-in mediation group. There are many benefits of practicing family meditation: it's one more activity to do together, it's fulfilling, it's relaxing, and it tightens the family bond. It is also a great way to introduce your children to spirituality, stress reduction, and contemplation. These seeds of meditation, planted in a child's early life, can sprout when they're adults and provide them with another coping mechanism. Also, keep in mind that sometimes family life can be stressful, and meditation is a powerful tool for cutting down stress inside the home. Here are a couple of simple, short meditations for the entire family.

Family Meditation #1

Have everyone sit, cross-legged, in a circle with knees touching. If sitting cross-legged is uncomfortable for anyone, then everyone can sit on chairs in a circle. Instruct everyone to close their eyes and take a few deep inhalations and exhalations. Next lead your meditation group in chanting "OM" three times in unison. Chanting OM is a way of synchronizing the family energies. Finally, invite everyone in the circle to meditate on family gratefulness specifically by saying to themselves, "I am grateful for . . . our home . . . my brother . . . my father . . . my sister . . . our car, etc."

Family Meditation #2

Have everyone sit, cross-legged, in a circle with knees touching. If sitting on the floor is completely uncomfortable for some family members, then everyone can sit on chairs in a circle. Instruct all to close their eyes and take a few deep inhalations and exhalations. Next lead your meditation group in chanting "OM" three times in unison. Finally, have the members do this lovingkindess meditation for each person present:

> May (name the individual) be filled with joy.
> May (name the individual) be filled with peace.
> May (name the individual) be filled with courage.
> May (name the individual) be filled with hope.

Exhalation Meditation

Often, you can create a physical and emotional sense of calm, tranquility, and inner peace by conscious deep breathing, especially on the exhalation. Though breathing is an automatic response and done properly when you are first born, this is not the case when we're a few years older. In fact, most adults do not breathe properly or efficiently. It seems that tension, stress, diet, and other factors conspire together to limit the benefits of breathing. The word used in meditation for breath is *prana*, which means "life-force energy." In fact, in our English language, the word *inspiration* comes from the Latin "inspirato" which literally means "to breathe." Breath is linked to divinity and wisdom. Proper breathing brings energy (or the life-force) into the entire body system: muscles, heart, lungs, brain, and digestion and impacts our emotional and physical state. For the purpose of releasing tension and restoring relaxation, try this exhalation meditation.

- Sit quietly with the goal of making your exhalation twice as long as your inhalation. For example, you could begin by inhaling to a count of 3 and exhaling to a count of 6, or you could inhale to a count of 4 or 5 and exhale to a count of 8 or 10. What this does is ensure that all of the stale air hidden in the lungs is properly forced out, permitting more fresh air to enter upon exhalation.
- Do this for 60 seconds or so.
- Resume normal breathing for a few inhalations and exhalations.
- Return to the exhalation meditation for another minute or so.
- Intersperse your meditation time with normal breathing in between the intentional longer exhalation exercise.

MEDITATION MOTIVATOR

Learn the richness of solitude and quiet. That still small voice is yearning to be heard.
- Susan Jeffers

When You Are Feeling Discouraged, Give This Some Thought!

Take a moment to think about the meaning these words: "Water which is too pure has no fish." They are from the Ts'ai Ken T'an, a document written in the late 16th century by the Chinese philosopher Hong Zicheng. The words are a gentle reminder to be grateful for challenges in our lives because without them there isn't much to living. Too many times we want life to be perfect, smooth, and easy. Yet if that was the case, then there wouldn't be enough to keep us mentally, emotionally, physically, and spiritually alive and vibrant. The sentence about the too pure water is directed toward those who want life to be pure and sanitized, free of messiness, problems, and/or challenges. The words are a caution that the sanitized life is not worth living.

Likewise, the modern Korean Zen Master, Kyong Ho (1849-1912) makes the same case. Consider his wisdom:

Don't wish for perfect health. In perfect health, there is greed and wanting. So an ancient said, 'Make good medicine from the suffering of sickness.'

Don't hope for a life without problems. An easy life results in a judgmental and lazy mind. So an ancient once said, 'Accept the anxieties and difficulties of this life.'

Don't expect your practice to be always clear of obstacles. Without hindrances the mind that seeks enlightenment may be burnt out. So an ancient once said, 'Attain deliverance in disturbances.'

Don't expect to practice hard and not experience the weird. Hard practice that evades the unknown makes for a weak commitment. So an ancient once said, 'Help hard practice by befriending every demon.'

Don't expect to finish doing something easily. If you happen to acquire something easily, the will is made weaker. So an ancient once said, 'Try again and again to complete what you are doing.'

Make friends, but don't expect any benefit for yourself. Friendship only for oneself harms trust. So an ancient once said, 'Have an enduring friendship with purity in heart.'

Don't expect others to follow your direction. When it happens that others go along with you, it results in pride. So an ancient once said, 'Use your will to bring peace between people.'

Expect no reward for an act of charity. Expecting something in return leads to a scheming mind. So an ancient once said, 'Throw false spirituality away like a pair of old shoes.'

Meditations to Center

Meditation on the Buddhist Eightfold Path

One of the core teachings of the Buddha is the Eightfold Path. For us to be centered and grounded, Buddha stressed these eight *rights*:

- right understanding;
- right purpose;
- right speech;
- right action;
- right livelihood;
- right effort;
- right mindfulness; and
- right concentration.

This ancient teaching of the Buddha makes an excellent framework for a number of meditations for becoming more centered, grounded, and skillful in life.

Eightfold Path Meditation for Self-awareness

This meditation can be spread over eight days doing one path each day. Those who grew up Catholic may recognize this process a similar to the Catholic "examination of conscience" meditation process.

- Begin by taking a few deep inhalations and exhalations before proceeding to mediate on the questions in each of the eight paths.
- Pause and remain silent for a few breaths after mediating on a path.

- Some people find it helpful to write down any insights gained as a result of the meditation.

Right Understanding Meditation

- Do I listen or simply hear?
- Do I listen compassionately, without judgment?
- After listening, do I truly understand?
- Do I listen compassionately to others? After hearing them, am I able to walk in their shoes and truly understand?

Right Purpose Meditation

- Am I living an authentic life?
- Do I experience fulfillment and joy?
- Is my life purposeful?

Right Speech Meditation

- Where did my words injure?
- Where did my words inspire?
- What can I learn from those two experiences?

Right Action Meditation

- Do I respond or react to situations?
- Are my actions skillful or awkward?
- Do my actions produce happy or unhappy results?

Right Livelihood Meditation

- Am I proud of my work?

- Is my work satisfying?
- Does my work make the planet a better place?

Right Effort Meditation

- Am I reliable?
- Do I do my best?
- Am I a person who follows through on promises and plans?

Right Mindfulness Meditation

- Am I an optimist or a cynic?
- Are my thoughts mainly hopeful or despairing?
- Can I see the good and the potential in everyone and everything?

Right Concentration Meditation

- Is my mind easily influenced?
- Am I easily distracted?
- Is my mind clear and calm when under pressure?

Eightfold Path Meditation for Improving Relationships

The Buddha's teaching can also be effectively applied in improving relationships. It is especially useful for people who feel they have no success in relationships or that they repeatedly make poor choices in life partners. Before making a serious commitment to a relationship, use this meditation to step back and cultivate deeper awareness.

Ask yourself these questions:

- Right understanding: Do we have common core values?
- Right purpose: Does this person have healthy, wholesome life goals?
- Right speech: Is this individual clear and direct in communication?
- Right action: Is this person honest, trustworthy, reliable, and persevering?
- Right livelihood: Does this individual have a healthy work ethic?
- Right effort: Is this person easily discouraged and defeated?
- Right mindfulness: Does this person do inner the work of reflection?
- Right concentration: Is this individual's mind restless or relaxed?

MEDITATION MOTIVATOR

Learn to be quiet enough to hear the genuine within yourself so that you can hear it in others.
- Marian Edelman

Meditation for Dealing with Difficulty

Meditating can help anyone deal with the numerous difficulties of life—an obnoxious co-worker, a tyrannical boss, a disappointing relationship, etc.—because it helps one become centered and understand people and situations from a more balanced perspective.

Directions:

- Sit comfortably and quietly.
- Take several deep inhalations and exhalations.
- Begin breathing normally.
- Review the difficulty you are facing. Notice how it is or has been affecting your body, mind, emotions, and spirit.
- Continue by asking yourself these types of questions, listening carefully to answers which emerge:
  o How have I responded or reacted to this difficulty?
  o Have I been skillful or careless?
  o Have I increased my own suffering?
  o What does this difficulty ask me to do?
  o What can I learn from this difficulty?
  o Is there a silver lining in this difficulty?

A meditation for difficulty can and ought to be done several times over several days because answers or openings often are realized gradually.

Meditations to Connect

A Dalai Lama Self-Awareness Meditation

This meditation is reported to be favored by the Dalai Lama and one he does frequently. It will help you develop a great inner connection, empowering you to see objectively what takes place with you and in you day by day. Begin the meditation by looking back over the previous week (seven days) of your life and ask yourself these questions, one by one, stopping to ponder each one before proceeding to the next one:

- What did I receive?
- What did I give?
- What difficulties and problems did I cause? As you review these, simply acknowledge them without harsh judgment. Learn from them by adding the resolve not to be a repeat offender.

Chakra Balancing Meditation

Here's a universal experience. You meet someone for the first time and are instantly drawn to them.   You find the person interesting, fascinating, pleasant, and naturally comfortable to be with. In this person's presence, you are instantly relaxed. On the other hand, there have been times when you have met a person and were intuitively put off by the individual. For reasons you couldn't immediately articulate, you found that individual boring, unpleasant, perhaps obnoxious and even offensive. It was simply a person with whom you couldn't establish a comfort zone. The East explains that the reason we all have those experiences is this: all living things are filled with energy and experience that energy in one way or another, knowingly or unknowingly. Our auras and chakras are interacting with the auras and chakras of others.

Chakra is a Sanskrit word which means wheel or disk. Eastern sages teach that chakras are vital energy centers flowing through the nerves up and down the spinal column and up to the head. Picture a spiraling vortex, a whirling mass of water or air that sucks everything near it toward its center. Chakras are often described as spinning vortices channeling cosmic energy. These energies are considered part of our connection with the divine or a higher consciousness. Most often people talk about the seven main chakras:

1. root chakra, located at the base of the spine;
2. sacral chakra, located in the lower abdomen (or 2 inches below the navel);
3. navel chakra;
4. heart chakra;
5. throat chakra;
6. third eye chakra, located between the eye brows and slightly above;
7. crown chakra, located at the very top of the head.

When the chakras operate at optimum—that is, when we experience greatest unity of the lower self with the Higher Self—we experience physical, emotional, and spiritual well-being. On the other hand, when that energy is blocked or interrupted, then we are less connected to the divine energy or the higher self; the result is confusion, emotional difficulty, and illness.

Here is a chakra meditation, designed to restore body/mind balance. Begin by reading the explanation of each chakra. Then go on to do a brief chakra meditation.

Root Chakra

The root or base chakra is located at the perineum at the base of the spine. This chakra is focused on basic survival needs: breathing, shelter, safety, and the health of our physical body.

Focus of Meditation:

Is this chakra out of balance in my life because I place too much emphasis upon material wealth, status, power, and possessions?

Second Chakra

The belly chakra is located in the lower abdomen and controls creativity—artistic, intellectual, and physical creativity as in our sexual energy. When it is free and unblocked, people experience passion and enthusiasm for living. Chakra imbalance in this area can often be seen in addictions and compulsions.

Focus of Meditation:

Is this chakra out of balance in my life because I am overly focused on satisfying physical desires? Do I struggle with addictive behavior?

Third Chakra

The navel or solar plexus chakra is center of our emotional life. It drives our self-esteem and self-confidence.

Focus of Meditation:

Is this chakra balanced? Can I act on my conviction and move forward in spite of resistance and criticism, or am I overly sensitive to the reactions of others, easily discouraged, and unable to maintain a course of action?

Fourth Chakra

The heart chakra is concerned with self-acceptance and compassionate living.

Focus of Meditation:

Am I compassionate, kind, loving, willing and able to reach out to others who are suffering? Or am I out of balance and unable to freely express kindness, love, and compassion?

Fifth Chakra:

The throat chakra controls creativity, self-expression, and communication—both verbal and nonverbal.

Focus of Meditation:

Is my throat chakra balanced? Do I communicate my feelings, thoughts, ideas and needs without bombarding or overwhelming others? Or is this chakra out of balance, causing me to be over-talkative and an energy vampire to others?

Sixth Chakra:

Often called the "third eye" chakra, the sixth chakra is located just above and between the eyebrows. It deals with imagination, intuition, imagination.

Focus of Meditation:

Do I trust my intuition and "read"/see people accurately? Is this chakra balanced allowing me to see things clearly? Or is it out of balance causing me to have distorted views and perceptions?

Seventh Chakra:

Located at the top of the head, the crown chakra deals with self-realization and inner knowledge. It is regarded as the key link between the human self and the higher self and is the area from which our spirituality emerges. The seventh chakra of all mystics and yogis is highly developed.

Focus of Meditation:

Am I moving on a spiritual path? Or am I person with limited spiritual appreciation and more focused on amassing material things?

Chakra Energy-Opening Meditation

There are times when our physical, emotional, and mental energies are very low or even being blocked. To open chakra energies, try this color chakra visualization meditation.

Begin by taking some deep inhalations and exhalations to release stress held in the body. Then move through the seven chakras this way:

1. Focus your attention on the first chakra at the base of the spine. Visualize a red flower slowly opening. See that red flower energy filling the base of your spine.
2. Focus your attention on the second chakra in the lower abdomen about two inches below the navel. Visualize an orange flower slowly opening. See that orange flower energy filling your lower abdomen.
3. Focus your attention on the navel chakra. Visualize a yellow flower slowly opening. See that yellow flower energy filling the area around your navel.
4. Focus your attention on the heart chakra. Visualize a green flower slowly opening. See that green flower energy filling your heart and the surrounding area.
5. Focus your attention on the throat chakra. Visualize a blue flower slowly opening. See that blue flower energy filling the area around your throat and neck.
6. Focus your attention on the third eye chakra. Visualize an indigo flower slowly opening. See that indigo flower

energy filling the area between your eyebrows and the forehead.

7. Focus your attention on the crown chakra. Visualize a purple flower slowly opening. See that purple flower energy filling your head.

8. Conclude by focusing and soaking in the rainbow beauty of your chakras.

MEDITATION MOTIVATOR

Solve all your problems through meditation.
Exchange unprofitable religious speculations for actual God-contact.
- Paramhansa Yogananda

Meditation for Radiating Peace and Joy

We can connect more deeply with others and with ourselves by simply choosing to be transmitters of peace and joy. A good time to do this is with a morning meditation before your day gets under way.   Begin by taking some deep inhalations and exhalations to release stress held in the body. Then try this basic five-minute meditation before you step outside your home:

My mind is filled with peace.
I radiate peace to everyone I meet.
My spirit is filled with joy.
I radiate joy to everyone I meet.

Morning Meditation for Greeting a New Day

You can use meditation to set an intention for a new day. Upon awakening, take some deep inhalations and exhalations to begin. Then as you sit on your bed in a comfortable meditation position, do this meditation:

Today
> May my actions be kind.
> May my words be encouraging.
> May they be beneficial.
> May I be of service.

Navajo Meditation for Inner Peace

The following is actually a prayer from the Navajo Native American tradition. However, it can easily be used as a meditation for cultivating greater inner peace. Before beginning this meditation, remember to take a few deep inhalations and exhalations and then return to normal breathing. Then simply repeat the following five lines over and over as a mantra:

Before me—peaceful.
Behind me—peaceful.
Under me—peaceful.
Over me—peaceful.
Around me—peaceful.

Part Four:

Five-Minute Meditations to Resurrect Your Spirit in Times of Trouble, Trauma, and Trial

Focus: Be the master of your mind, not mastered by your mind!

Meditation is an invaluable tool when facing life's challenges. Meditators are noted for their ability to achieve the following:

- remain calm in crisis;
- be focused on solutions, not problems;
- remain optimistic and hopeful;
- react more quickly and efficiently to a stressful event;
- possess deepened will power;
- have reduced feelings of fear;
- manage their minds rather than be managed by the mind;
- live in the present moment;
- display greater inner-directedness; and/or
- bring body, mind, and spirit into harmony.

Remember that meditation is a tool for becoming master of your mind, rather than being mastered by your mind. The mind, actually your mind, can be your greatest ally or your greatest opponent. Here's one study which reveals the negative power of the mind. A group of students were told that a mild electric current would be sent through their brains and that it might cause a headache in some of them. Each one was fitted with electrodes but no electricity was applied. Nevertheless, a full 70% said they suffered headaches "after the electricity passed through their brains."

Dealing with Life's Changes and Challenges

Everything on our planet is subject to change. Rivers change. Lakes change. Trees change. Even the mountains change. And change will come to every single person. One day you have a job; the next day you've been downsized. One day you're healthy; the next day you have a diagnosis of serious illness. One day you're happy; the next day you're depressed. One day you're married; the next day you've been widowed. Changes come, some gradually, others suddenly.

Some changes are welcome, but many are not. Buddhism teaches that our suffering results from our inability or unwillingness to adjust our lives to the change which has come. When change comes, we suffer more deeply when we cling to the way we wish our lives were rather than adapt to the way it really is.

Meditation is invaluable because change is inevitable. Use these meditations whenever it feels as though everything in your life is falling apart.

MEDITATION MOTIVATOR

When we meditate, we expand—
spreading our wings like a bird,
trying to enter consciously into Infinity, Eternity, and
Immortality,
welcoming them into our aspiring consciousness—
we see, feel, and grow into the entire universe of Light-Delight.
- Sri Chinmoy

Meditations to Soothe

Namaha Meditation

Namaha is a Sanskrit word meaning "Not me" or "Not mine" or "It's out of my hands." It is a reminder that we are not the ones in control, and it is ideally used in meditation for those times when we experience disappointment because our plans and hopes are not working out. Here is how to do a "Namaha" meditation when you're feeling disappointed and discouraged. Before beginning this meditation, remember to take a few deep inhalations and exhalations and then return to normal breathing.

Inhale the sentence and exhale Namaha as you repeat these kinds of statements. You can repeat just one sentence or a combination of these.

> It's not about me—namaha.
> All is well—namaha.
> There is a greater plan—namaha.
> I have faith—namaha.
> A way will open—namaha.

Then as you continue to inhale and exhale, simply keep repeating "Namaha" and allowing its meaning and faith to penetrate your consciousness.

Here's how the Namaha Meditation worked for one woman. In her mid 50's the woman—Lynnette—had a cough that lasted several weeks. She went to her family practice doctor who examined her recommending more tests. When they came back, she was shocked to learn she had cancer in her lungs, which had already migrated into her brain. Suddenly she had to sort out massive amounts of information about chemotherapy, radiation, and treatment at another city hospital that specialized in her type of cancer. Overwhelmed, she remembered the Namaha meditation she'd learned at her meditation group.

In the quiet and comfort of her home, Lynnette sat on her meditation cushion and adapted the meditation specifically for her situation:

> All will be well—namaha.
> All is well—namaha.
> There is a higher purpose—namaha.
> I have faith—namaha.
> One day at a time—namaha.

After placing her focus on this Namaha mediation for a few minutes, Lynnette said she felt calmer and more confident about dealing with her cancer diagnosis.

Healing Light Meditation

This is meditation designed to generate relaxation and healing:

- Sit comfortably, taking a few deep inhalations and exhalations.
- Begin to breathe normally.
- Start to imagine that your body is filling up with light beginning at your feet.
    - See that light moving slowly up your body.
    - Feel the light releasing tension and relaxing the muscles in your legs, in your arms, around your chest, in your neck.
    - Imagine that any illness, disease, or pain in any part of your body has a dark shape, a shadow.
    - Visualize and feel yourself directing the light slowly to that area of illness, disease, or pain.

- o Continue directing light toward the area which is giving you pain and discomfort. See the light penetrating that shadow area.
- Conclude by repeating:
  - o The light is healing my body.
  - o The light is renewing my health.
  - o The light is restoring my vitality.

Greek Philosopher Meditation

The ancient Greek philosopher, Heraclitus of Ephesus said that impermanence and change are constant: "Everything flows and nothing abides; everything gives way, and nothing stays fixed." His wisdom can be the foundation of this meditation that is based on your breath inhalations and exhalations:

Inhale and say, "Everything flows."
Exhale and say, "And nothing abides."
Inhale and say, "Everything gives way."
Exhale and say, "And nothing stays fixed."

Repeat these over and over as you connect each phrase to your breath.

Meditation on Change

This meditation can help you view change with more optimism and less fear. Before beginning this meditation, remember to take a few deep inhalations and exhalations and then return to normal breathing.

The key to this meditation is to repeat three short, positive sentences as you would repeat mantras. Recite each sentence as a breath—an inhalation and exhalation is one breath. Continue repeating the three sentences you've chosen for five minutes. Choose one of the following examples:

Change comes to everyone.
Change is my opportunity for growth.
Change will bring me new perspectives.

Change helps me be more flexible.
Change empowers me to practice resilience.
Change creates new ways of thinking for me.

Change is teaching me new lessons.
Change reminds me I'm not always in control.
Change empowers me to trust.

Change gives me important choices for responding.
Change helps me surrender or relinquish control.
Change develops and deepens my personality.

Change helps me rebuild.
Change helps me regroup.
Change can be good.

MEDITATION MOTIVATOR

Meditation speaks. It speaks in silence.
It reveals. It reveals to the aspirant that matter and spirit are
one,
quantity and quality are one,
the immanent and the transcendent are one.
It reveals that life can never be the mere existence of seventy or
eighty years between birth and death, but is, rather,
Eternity
itself.
- Sri Chinmoy

Sacred Word Meditation

Many find it helpful to meditate by reciting a sacred word as
the entire focus of their meditation. A sacred word is any word
which is meaningful to you and brings a sense of stability to
you. Some examples of sacred words include:

Love	Clarity	Peace	Wisdom
Joy	Acceptance	Life	Forgiveness
Now	Oneness	Yes	Surrender
Calm	Illumination	Happiness	Inspiration
Faith	Creativity	Hope	Patience
Kindness	Humility	Gentleness	Gratitude
Compassion	Release	Wonder	Awe

Find your sacred word. Here's how to use it in meditation.

- If your sacred word is *peace*, then, as you inhale, say, "Peace in," and as you exhale, say "Peace out."
- If your sacred word is *hope*, then as you inhale, say, "Hope in," and as you exhale, say "Hope out."

Continue for five minutes.

Simple Walking Meditation

Walking meditation is commonly practiced by the Buddhist monks of Southeast Asia. It's a great way to combine meditation, exercise, and being outdoors all at the same time. Walking meditation is also ideal for releasing tension because it combines physical activity with mind focus so you can burn calories as well as stress. Here is a basic walking mediation done by counting the steps:

- Begin walking at your normal pace.
- Start a count from one to four, counting each time your left foot comes down. For example: 1, 2, 3, 4.
- Then add one number to the original 4 count and continue adding until you reach 10 like this:
  - After the first round of 4, continue with the left foot coming down: 1, 2, 3, 4, 5.
  - Return to one but add an additional count: 1, 2, 3, 4, 5, 6, etc.
  - Do this until you reach ten with the left foot.
  - Now take a few normal steps and resume the meditation using the right foot to count.
  - Alternate back and forth from left foot to right foot, doing walking meditation.

Five minutes is a good start but always feel free to add more meditative time to your walk. Just remember to focus and not enter automatic counting.

Always remember there is a Buddha in your mirror!

Whenever Morihei Ueshiba, Japanese mystic and founder of the martial art, Akido, encountered students who seemed lost about their purpose in life, he told them, "You are here to realize your inner divinity and manifest your innate enlightenment."

Though he's correct, tapping into our inner divinity and acting upon our innate enlightenment is difficult because we have expended great effort to cover up our divinity. We often do this because of life's threats and cruelties. Rather than remain open, available, and, therefore, vulnerable, we protect ourselves from potential harm and injury. There is an interesting historical analogy to this psychological defense mechanism.

Inside a large temple north of Thailand's ancient capital, Sukotai, there once stood an enormous ancient clay Buddha. Though not considered a particularly refined work of Thai Buddhist art, the clay Buddha was carefully cared for over a 500-year period. Gradually it came to be revered and honored for its survival and longevity. During those 500 years, the Buddha endured violent storms, invading armies, and changes of government. It was the one constant in an otherwise changing environment.

Then the monks who looked after the temple noticed the statue had begun to crack. As the weather became hotter and drier, the crack became so wide that a curious monk took his flashlight to peer inside. He was stunned to see that behind the clay, was glittering gold. Chipping and scraping away the outside clay, temple residents discovered one of the largest gold images of Buddha ever created in Southeast Asia. Today the uncovered Golden Buddha draws crowds of pilgrims and tourists from all over Thailand and around the world. The monks assume the Golden Buddha was covered in plaster and clay to protect it during times of conflict and unrest.

There is something of us in that story. We are born with divinity inside, but threatening situations of all kinds— emotional, spiritual, intellectual, and physical—have prompted us to cover up our innate divine nature. Each one of us needs to look carefully at ourselves and see that beneath the clay and plaster is original goodness, compassion, and divinity. In the East this is called our Buddha nature. Even Judaism and Christianity offer a similar thought. The book of Genesis notes that "God created man in his own image, in the image of God he created him; male and female" (Genesis 1:27). Jesus taught that "the kingdom of God is within you" (Luke 17:21), and twice in his writings, St. Paul speaks of our inner divinity. In Corinthians 6:19, he said, "Your body is a temple of the Holy Spirit, who is in you, whom you have received from God." In another writing, he reminded early followers of the "Christ in you" (Colossians 1:27).

Every time you look into a mirror, try reminding yourself that you are looking at a Buddha, at a Christ. See and sense your inner nobility, dignity, beauty, and divinity. Rather than live out of a limited, fearful, impoverished identity, live as a person who is on an enlightened path. See yourself a part of the Divine or the Larger Self as you practice meditation. That way you will be a blessing to those around you in your part of the world.

MEDITATION MOTIVATOR

If you meditate, sooner or later you will come upon love.
If you meditate deeply, sooner or later you will start feeling a
tremendous love
arising in you that you have never known before.

- Osho

Meditations to Sustain

Buddhist Lovingkindness Meditation

As a meditator, you will also want to be mindful for others when everything for them falls apart. When you know someone—family member, friend, neighbor, work colleague, or even a friend of a friend—who is going through a hard time, such as an illness, separation, divorce, bereavement, incarceration, job loss, etc. , offer this traditional Buddhist Lovingkindness meditation on their behalf. It can sustain them in their time of struggle.

This meditation is done in three phases, casting a wide net of loving kindness. Before beginning this meditation, remember to take a few deep inhalations and exhalations and then return to normal breathing.

1. You will begin the meditation by focusing on yourself.
2. Then move on to focus on people you love.

3. Finally focus upon the individual who is experiencing difficulty.

The reason for beginning with yourself and people you love is build within your spirit deep compassionate and loving feelings. Then, that same depth of compassion and love, once established, is sent out to the person facing difficulty.

Here is the Buddhist lovingkindness meditation:

May I be healthy.
May I be happy.
May I be safe.
May I be free of suffering.

May (name of loved one) be healthy.
May (name of loved one) be happy.
May (name of loved one) be safe.
May (name of loved one) be free of suffering.

May (name of person in crisis) be healthy.
May (name of person in crisis) be happy.
May (name of person in crisis) be safe.
May (name of person in crisis) be free of suffering.

One word of explanation about this meditation: some people are confused about the last phrase "to be free of suffering." In Buddhist psychology there is an enormous difference between pain and suffering. In fact, a common Buddhist teaching states that "Pain is inevitable; suffering is optional." The Buddhist view is that everyone will experience pain, but suffering is an extra layer we add onto our pain by our attitude. For example, if a person is diagnosed with a life threatening illness, that can cause them emotional pain. However, the person adds to this burden by an attitude which conveys bitterness or entitlement by constantly thinking or saying things like these: "Why me?" "Why do these things always happen to me?" "Life isn't fair." "I never get any breaks." When we say "May Deborah be free of suffering," we are asking the universe (or the Divine) to free her from adding suffering, which is a self-inflicted wound. The pain she is experiencing is enough.

Tonglen Meditation for One Who Suffers

Another meditative technique you can offer for someone suffering is called Tonglen. This is a Tibetan Buddhist practice. The word "tonglen" means "sending and receiving" or "giving and taking." Before beginning this meditation, remember to take a few deep inhalations and exhalations and then return to normal breathing. This meditation is done in six steps:

1. Place the person firmly and clearly in your mind.
2. Imagine all of the details connected to the person's condition.
3. Visualize all aspects of the person's distress—physical pain, emotional upset, spiritual crisis, feelings of fear, anxiety, anger, depression, etc.
4. Inhaling, see all of that distress being absorbed in a dark gray ball of smoke. As it enters your healthy system, see that dark gray ball of distress being transformed into a gentle white cloud against a blue sky.
5. Exhaling, visualize a healing light flowing from you directly to the person in distress. Keep focusing on the person and sending that person pure energy of peace, healing, kindness, compassion, joy.

6. Continue taking in the gray and sending out the white for this person.

Tonglen Meditation for When You Suffer

A tonglen meditation can also be done when you are the one suffering and in difficulty. The pattern is the same—sending and receiving, giving and taking. Before beginning this meditation, remember to take a few deep inhalations and exhalations and then return to normal breathing. Follow these steps to practice a tonglen meditation for yourself:

1. Place yourself and your difficulty clearly in your mind.
2. Avoid judging, blaming, or criticizing yourself.
3. Breathe in the issue visualizing it as a dark gray ball of smoke.
4. Then visualize the dark gray ball being transformed via your breath into a soft, white cloud in a bright, blue sky.

Finish by gently offering these loving kindness thoughts to yourself:

May fear be lifted.
May anger be dissolved.
May resentment be released.
May peace and joy be present in me.

MEDITATION MOTIVATOR

When we raise ourselves through meditation to what unites us with the spirit,
we quicken something within us that is eternal and unlimited by birth and death.
Once we have experienced this eternal part in us,
we can no longer doubt its existence.
Meditation is thus the way to knowing and beholding the eternal, indestructible, essential center of our being.
- Rudolf Steiner

Forgiveness Meditation—Forgiving Others

Being alive means being hurt by others from time to time. People close to us sometimes bring us pain by their words and deeds. By their actions, intentional or unintentional, we can be left feeling abused, betrayed, and/or abandoned. Rather than harbor ill-will, anger, and resentment toward them, we can help ourselves by working toward forgiving the wrong-doer. Ajahn Chah, a Thai Buddhist meditation master rightly taught:

> If you let go a little,
> you will have a little happiness.
> If you let go a lot,
> you will have a lot of happiness.
> If you let go completely,
> you will be free.

Before beginning this forgiveness meditation, remember to take a few deep inhalations and exhalations and then return to normal breathing. Here is the forgiveness meditation to utilize when you need to forgive another person. It's done in four stages:

Stage #1: Focus upon yourself and say:

> May I be filled with peace.
> May I be filled with love.
> May I be filled with joy.
> May I be healthy and whole.

Stage #2: Focus on someone you love and appreciate. This could be a family member or friend. Name and visualize that person in your mind and say:

> May (name) be filled with peace.
> May (name) be filled with love.
> May (name) be filled with joy.
> May (name) be healthy and whole.

Stage #3: Focus on someone you feel neutral about. This could be bank teller, store clerk, a teacher. Name and visualize that person in your mind and say:

> May (name) be filled with peace.
> May (name) be filled with love.
> May (name) be filled with joy.
> May (name) be healthy and whole.

Stage #4: Focus on the person who has hurt you or caused you difficulty. Visualize that individual in your mind and say:

> May (name) be filled with peace.
> May (name) be filled with love.
> May (name) be filled with joy.

May (name) be healthy and whole.

Allow your feelings of goodwill spread throughout your mind, your emotions, your spirit. Remind yourself that you are forgiving the individual, releasing all hurt and pain, and setting yourself free from anger and resentment.

Forgiveness Meditation #1—Forgiving Yourself

Sometimes we are the source of hurt and pain to another person. Whenever you recognize you have been the one causing this, turn to meditation rather than spending time in regret, guilt, and personal disappointment. Before beginning this meditation, remember to take a few deep inhalations and exhalations and then return to normal breathing. Now bring to mind the person you have injured and meditate this way:

I am sorry for what I have done.
My actions came out of ignorance or fear or anger.
I feel sorrow and remorse.
I am sorry.

Repeat this several times, and as you do, soften your attitude toward yourself. If it is appropriate, you might consider writing the person you have injured, expressing the same words you used in this meditation.

Forgiveness Meditation #2—Forgiving Yourself

Use this meditation to release yourself from guilt and regret over anything you've done which caused pain and/or injury. Before beginning this meditation, remember to take a few deep inhalations and exhalations and then return to normal breathing.

May I forgive myself for hurting another
either intentionally or unintentionally.
May I forgive myself for hurting myself
either intentionally or unintentionally.
    I forgive myself,
    I forgive myself,
    I forgive myself.

MEDITATION MOTIVATOR

Real peace is always unshakeable ... Bliss is unchanged by
gain or loss.
- Yogi Bhajan

Meditations to Settle

Meditation on Fullness

An effective meditation for settling mind and spirit involves using words which end in "full." Some examples are thankful, beautiful, wonderful, peaceful, grateful, blissful, bountiful, playful, and graceful. Before beginning this meditation, remember to take a few deep inhalations and exhalations and then return to normal breathing.

- Pick three "full" words for your meditation.
- Inhale on the first part of the word.
- Always exhale on the "full."
- For example:
  - Peaceful
    - Inhale *peace.*
    - Exhale *full.*
  - Wonderful

106

- Inhale *wonder.*
- Exhale *full.*
  o Beautiful
    - Inhale *beauty.*
    - Exhale *full.*

The purpose of this meditation is to "fill" you with peace, wonder, and beauty.

The 40-Breath Counting Meditation

Begin this 40-Breath Meditation by sitting comfortably, gently closing your eyes, and taking several deep inhalations and exhalations.

- Now scan your body and relax any part that is tense.
- Count your breaths—an inhalation-exhalation is one count.
- Count up to 40.
- As thoughts enter your mind, don't argue or judge them. Simply acknowledge them and continue counting.
- When you reach 40, continue the same process counting backwards.
- Conclude by repeating a word or short phrase that you intend to be mindful of during the rest of the day, such as love, joy, praise, peace, compassion, patience, etc.

Three-Point Personal Check-In Practice

Before beginning this three-point check-in meditation, remember to take a few deep inhalations and exhalations and then return to normal breathing. Use this mediation to gently tune in to yourself and become aware of what's happening to you and inside you. The simple act of placing your attention on your head, heart, and body in this way is calming and centering.

In my head: what am I thinking?
In my heart: what am I feeling?
In my body: what am I sensing?

Meditation for Inviting a Specific Quality into Your Life

Before beginning this meditation, remember to take a few deep inhalations and exhalations and then return to normal breathing. What quality do you feel you would like to increase in your life right now? Identify it in one or two words. Then breathe that quality into your life and exhale its opposite. For example:

Breathe love in and loneliness out.
Breathe peace in and anxiety out.
Breathe calm in and stress out.
Breathe abundance in and lack out.
Breathe forgiveness in and anger out.
Breathe hope in and despair out.
Freedom in and restriction out.
Breathe courage in and fear out.
Breathe wisdom in and confusion out.
Breathe tranquility in and nervousness out.
Breathe humility in and ego out.
Breathe compassion in and indifference out.
Breathe a positive relationship in and aloneness out.

Meditation Focusing on Gratitude

A thankful person is a peaceful person. Those who know how to give and receive gratitude experience greater harmony and balance in life. Before beginning this two-part gratitude meditation, remember to take a few deep inhalations and exhalations and then return to normal breathing.

> *Part 1:* In your mind go back over the last few months and bring to your memory people who thanked you for something you said or did. Relive each encounter specifically remembering how it felt to be appreciated.

> *Part 2:* In your mind go back over the last few months and bring to your memory people you could thank. Mentally, go and thank various individuals. Imagine how they feel when you thank them and show appreciation.

Conclude by noticing how it feels to be the one receiving and the one extending gratitude.

Here are a couple of thoughts which can deepen your interest in doing a gratitude meditation. Zen teacher John Tarrant reminds us: "You're alive. That's good. Lower the bar."

Making a similar emphasis on gratitude, the Buddha himself became a cheerleader for his monks when they were discouraged and found it hard to express gratitude. The Buddha reminded them:

> Let us rise up and be thankful,
> for if we didn't learn a lot today,
> at least we learned a little,

and if we didn't learn a little,
at least we didn't get sick,
and if we got sick, at least we didn't die,
so let us all be thankful.

MEDITATION MOTIVATOR

*To meditate does not mean to fight with a problem. To
meditate means to observe.
Your smile proves it.
It proves that you are being gentle with yourself
that the sun of awareness is shining in you, that you have
control of your situation.
You are yourself, and you have acquired some peace.*
- Thich Nhat Hanh

Meditation Focusing on Anonymous Kindnesses Received

Before beginning either of these meditations, remember to take a few deep inhalations and exhalations and then return to normal breathing. This meditation will deepen your gratitude toward people you don't know and may never have seen, yet such individuals show you kindness anonymously. Here's one way to practice this meditation:

1. Think of the supermarket where you buy your groceries.
2. Picture the many goods available to you in that store.
3. In your mind begin to go over the many people involved in making those products available to you. For example, the farmer, the truck driver, the person who unloads the truck, the person who orders the products,

the one who brings them into the store, the person who does the shelving, etc.

4. Be grateful for each of these individuals.

Here's another way to do a meditation focus on anonymous kindnesses received:

1. Think of your clothes closet with the wide variety of clothing there on hangers.
2. Put into your mind one of your favorite items of clothing (a sweater, a pair of shoes, a suit, a hat, a belt).
3. In your mind begin to go over the many people involved in making that one item available to you. For example, if it's a sweater, bring to mind a rancher who raised the sheep which produced the wool, the person who sheared the sheep cultivating the wool, the factory worker who spun the wool turning it into a sweater, the shipping clerk who processed the order, the buyer, the clerk who carefully displayed the sweater, etc.
4. Be grateful for each of these individuals and their roles in creating your sweater.

The Seventy-Two Labors Meditation

In the Vietnamese Zen tradition, there is a practice often done prior to a meal in which gratitude is expressed for the "72 innumerable labors" which were required for the food to be available at a dining table. That exercise is designed to make us aware how interdependent we are on one another. Recalling the "72 innumerable labors" effectively challenges our tendencies to feel entitled or unappreciative. Here's how to do it:

1. Sit comfortably taking a few deep inhalations and exhalations before returning to normal breathing.
2. Bring to mind a modern convenience which is indispensable to you. (For me, it's my laptop computer.)
3. Begin thinking how important this item is to you and the many benefits it brings you.
4. Move on to focus, one by one, on the many individuals whose labor contributed to making the item which is indispensable in your life. With the computer, I would imagine the miner who dug and extracted the metals needed to construct the computer, the oil worker who drilled for and discovered the oil necessary to build plastic parts in the computer, the assembly workers who put the laptop together, the software engineers who create programs to run the laptop, the truck driver who delivered my laptop to a distribution facility, etc.
5. As you think of each person, express gratitude to all of these individuals for their gifts of labor.

Concluding Thought

A friend of mine spent seven years living and studying at an ashram in India. Periodically ashram leaders would conduct a sacred fire ceremony. The energy of the fire symbolizes the energy of the Divine, so worshippers gather around the fire with an intense focus upon the Divine as they place offerings into the fire while chanting mantras. The fire ceremony lasts many days, so my friend's job was to stoke the ashes through the night in order to keep the fire going. Without someone to stoke the ashes, the fire would simply dwindle out because of the suffocating weight of the ashes. Though there were glowing embers buried beneath the top ashes, the pit had to be stirred in order for the flame to glow.

Our lives are symbolized by that fire pit. Within each of us is a light; however, the stresses and strains of life are like ashes which cover up and hide the light. Consequently, people begin to look outside themselves for solutions, for happiness, for meaning. Yet, because all of us have that inner light, inner wisdom, or the divine within us, all we truly need to do is stir the "ashes" of life which have been layered upon us. Meditation is the stirring tool we use to access our inner light and wisdom.

Everything you need for greater health, harmony, and happiness is within your reach because it is within!

MEDITATION MOTIVATOR

To become different from what we are, we must have some awareness of what we are.
- Bruce Lee

About the Author

Victor M Parachin

Victor Parachin grew up in Canada and graduated from the University of Toronto School of Theology and is an ordained minister.

Victor is a meditation teacher and yoga educator. He and his partner, Janet, are directors of Yoga Spirit Academy, a yoga teacher training school in Tulsa, Oklahoma.

He is the author of numerous books on Eastern spirituality.

Other Books By Ozark Mountain Publishing, Inc.

Dolores Cannon
Conversations with Nostradamus,
　　Volume I, II, III
Jesus and the Essenes
They Walked with Jesus
Between Death and Life
A Soul Remembers Hiroshima
Keepers of the Garden.
The Legend of Starcrash
The Custodians
The Convoluted Universe - Book One,
　　Two, Three, Four
Five Lives Remembered
The Three Waves of Volunteers and the
　　New Earth
Stuart Wilson & Joanna Prentis
The Essenes - Children of the Light
Power of the Magdalene
Beyond Limitations
Atlantis and the New Consciousness
The Magdalene Version
O.T. Bonnett, M.D./Greg Satre
Reincarnation: The View from Eternity
What I Learned After Medical School
Why Healing Happens
M. Don Schorn
Elder Gods of Antiquity
Legacy of the Elder Gods
Gardens of the Elder Gods
Reincarnation...Stepping Stones of Life
Aron Abrahamsen
Holiday in Heaven
Out of the Archives – Earth Changes
Sherri Cortland
Windows of Opportunity
Raising Our Vibrations for the New Age
Michael Dennis
Morning Coffee with God
God's Many Mansions
Nikki Pattillo
Children of the Stars
A Spiritual Evolution
Rev. Grant H. Pealer
Worlds Beyond Death
A Funny Thing Happened on the Way to
　　Heaven
Maiya & Geoff Gray-Cobb
Angels - The Guardians of Your Destiny
Seeds of the Soul
Sture Lönnerstrand
I Have Lived Before
Arun & Sunanda Gandhi
The Forgotten Woman
Claire Doyle Beland
Luck Doesn't Happen by Chance

James H. Kent
Past Life Memories As A Confederate
　　Soldier
Dorothy Leon
Is Jehovah An E.T
Justine Alessi & M. E. McMillan
Rebirth of the Oracle
Donald L. Hicks
The Divinity Factor
Christine Ramos, RN
A Journey Into Being
Mary Letorney
Discover The Universe Within You
Debra Rayburn
Let's Get Natural With Herbs
Jodi Felice
The Enchanted Garden
Susan Mack & Natalia Krawetz
My Teachers Wear Fur Coats
Ronald Chapman
Seeing True
Rev. Keith Bender
The Despiritualized Church
Vara Humphreys
The Science of Knowledge
Karen Peebles
The Other Side of Suicide
Antoinette Lee Howard
Journey Through Fear
Julia Hanson
Awakening To Your Creation
Irene Lucas
Thirty Miracles in Thirty Days
Mandeep Khera
Why?
Robert Winterhalter
The Healing Christ
James Wawro
Ask Your Inner Voice
Tom Arbino
You Were Destined to be Together
Maureen McGill & Nola Davis
Live From the Other Side
Anita Holmes
TWIDDERS
Walter Pullen
Evolution of the Spirit
Cinnamon Crow
Teen Oracle
Chakra Zodiac Healing Oracle
Jack Churchward
Lifting the Veil on the Lost Continent of
　　Mu
Guy Needler
The History of God
Beyond the Source – Book 1

For more information about any of the above titles, soon to be released titles,
or other items in our catalog, write or visit our website:
PO Box 754, Huntsville, AR 72740
www.ozarkmt.com

Other Books By Ozark Mountain Publishing, Inc.

Dee Wallace/Jarrad Hewett
The Big E
Dee Wallace
Conscious Creation
Natalie Sudman
Application of Impossible Things
Henry Michaelson
And Jesus Said – A Conversation
Victoria Pendragon
SleepMagic
Riet Okken
The Liberating Power of Emotions
Janie Wells
Payment for Passage
Dennis Wheatley
The Essential Dowsing Guide

For more information about any of the above titles, soon to be released titles,
or other items in our catalog, write or visit our website:
PO Box 754, Huntsville, AR 72740
www.ozarkmt.com